Amazing Fish Stories

by

Robert Ellis Cahill

Table of Contents

I. Good Fish and Bad Fish 7

II. Multi-armed Marvels 41

III. Man versus Shark 55

IV. Fishing for Food and Medicine 75

V. Deep Dark Sea 97

Photo by Ron Church

Dedication

This book is dedicated to my niece, Kristi Elizabeth (Gertrude) Cahill, a recent graduate of Salem State College, with a Bachelor of Science Degree in Biology. Her beauty is only surpassed by her brain, and being from a family of sea folks, we all hope that she – Goes Fish!

Photo by Paul Tzimouli

© Copyright Old Saltbox - 1996   ISBN – 1-889-193-00-3
COVER PHOTO: "The Fisherman," by an unknown artist. Photo by Steve Harwood.
Back cover photos by Ron Church and Paul Tzimoulis.

Tom Hubbel of Cayman Island, spears a hogfish for dinner.
Photo by Paul Tzimoulis

INTRODUCTION

This book is the result of some forty years of research. As a youth raised on and around the seashore of New England's Gold Coast — Salem and Marblehead, Massachusetts — my first and foremost interest was the sea and all its wonders. Scuba diving equipment was introduced to America in the early 1950's and my older brother Jim, being a former Navy Frogman, was the first to break the surface barrier of the North Atlantic to swim with the fish. I was seventeen years old at the time, and only because of my convenient availability, I was the second person in New England to join my brother in the depths. Needless to say, I was enthralled at what I saw beneath the waves. Cautious at first, I soon became relaxed and confident, exploring further and further into the depths, where no man had penetrated before. As I constantly encountered new denizens of the deep, I would study their habits and antics, and visit the local library to learn as much as I could about every specie.

Later in life I spent years diving and studying the sea life in the Red Sea, Caribbean and other fresh and salt bodies of water. Because of heart problems I was forced to give up my adventures in the sea some twenty years ago, yet my obsession with sea-creatures and their environment remains. The results of my experiences and study of fish I now share with you in this little book. I have tried to present here only the unique, bizarre, humorous and what I consider remarkable stories and information regarding these finny creatures, and their constant conflict with the most brutal of enemies — Man!

Good fish–the fantail file fish, with its file raised just above the eye, to lure smaller fish. Photo by Paul Tzimoulis

Bad fish–the lion fish is beautiful but deadly if touched.
Photo by Ron Church

I
GOOD FISH AND BAD FISH

Of the many classes of animals, including humans, that are in this world, over 60% of them are found underwater. The biggest, smallest and oldest animals are in the sea and up until one half billion years ago, all life was in the sea. Life itself began in the sea about two billion years ago and since that time the fish has become a very special animal, developed into approximately 40,000 known varieties and packaged by nature into about 1,000 different physical forms.

The largest fish is the whale shark, weighing several tons and measuring about 50 feet in length. The smallest is the goby, measuring about 1/3rd of an inch. The most common fish in the sea is one which most people have never seen. It is the bristle-mouth, which grows to a length of two to three inches and lives in the middle of the oceans. Probably the fish that is seen and eaten most frequently by humans is herring, of which there are 100 different species. Another popular fish is the black bass and in fact it is so popular that we have seen fit to give it 44 different names.

We humans have caused a great deal of confusion in the sea by giving the same fish many different names and at the same time, giving different species of fish the same name. For example: the fish called red drum by the people of New Jersey is called striped drum in New York and is given the name channel bass in the Carolinas. The red drum is called redfish in Florida, which confuses New England fishermen, for they catch redfish commercially, but the New England redfish belongs to a different family than the Florida redfish. Another fish that has a variety of names is the deadly but beautiful firefish. This six inch coral dweller lives in the tropics almost everywhere in the world and is also known as the lion fish, cobra fish, zebra fish, turkey fish and dragon fish.

Swimmers and divers must quickly learn to identify the feathery looking lion fish, for although it is not aggressive, it can kill anything or anyone who touches it. Its fins look like the colorful tail of a turkey and its dorsal fin resembles a lion's mane, but contained in that dorsal fin are 13 spines loaded with venom. The lion fish also has four venom-loaded stingers in its anal and ventral fins. I have met up with many of these deadly midgets while diving in the Red Sea and always gave them a wide berth. I also witnessed an Eritrean Arab suffer the after effects of being stung by a lion fish. He screeched in pain and even when his friends placed a hot iron on his swollen limb (a common Arab treatment for stings) the victim didn't mind the treatment half as much as he did the painful wound from the fish. Other natives informed me that those who are stung by the lion fish suffer an agonizing few days before they die.

There is also a so-called lion fish that lives in the South Atlantic that is actually a scorpion fish and a distant cousin to the lion fish mentioned above. The head and body of this ugly scorpion fish is covered with a hard, brown armor-like crust and also has a venom in it sharp spines, but it is not potent enough to kill humans. A West Coast cousin of the scorpion fish is the sculpin and its barbs are deadlier. The rosefish, a milder Asian relative, is colored bright orange, but otherwise looks like the scorpion fish and the West Indies scorpion has a bright yellow belly, but otherwise is a crusty brown. Probably the most feared of the scorpion fish family is the stonefish. It lives on and in the muddy bottom along the coasts of India, China, Japan and Australia. The sting of the stonefish has been compared to that of the cobra snake, for its venom attacks a human's nervous system. People who live through the sting of the stonefish suffer continuous fainting spells for two months or more.

Skates and stingrays which come in varying forms and sizes, have a barb or two near the base of their tail that can be dangerous to man. One type of Australian stingray has a eight inch barb and recently a skin-diver was jabbed in the heart by this barb and was killed. Usually however, it's a person wading in shallow water that accidentally steps on a stingray and gets a barb in the foot, suffering minor swelling of the foot and much pain. The sting of the diamond ray can cause vomiting, diarrhea and sometimes permanent paralysis. There is also a 24 inch spotted roundray that has a potent stinger and the say's-ray has a whip-like tail that is longer than its body and a long barb that can cause tremendous pain to its victim. One of the most dangerous rays is a fresh water species found in the Amazon River. The venom in its tail barb can cause immediate death. The large bat-ray has a dagger-like barb that contains a poison more potent than that of a rattle-snake. One bat-ray caught off California a few years ago weighed 200 lbs. and in Australian waters, one was caught that weighed close to 800 lbs. All the rayfish have been known to use their barbs to cut a fisherman's line when they are hooked. A ray will double up its body and using their barb like a knife, try to slice through the line and many times they are successful.

The manta ray, also called devil fish, the biggest of the ray family, is harmless. It can weigh well over a ton and although it was once greatly feared, today divers frolic in the water with it. The manta is also the only member of the ray family that doesn't spend its life hugging the ocean bottom. It often glides over the surface waters, slapping the waves with its 20-foot wing-like fins. Another black sheep of the ray family is the two to four-foot torpedo fish. It doesn't have a barbed tail, but instead nature provided it with a series of cells in its head that can generate an electric current capable of giving humans a severe shock.

Some 2,000 years ago, Roman doctors had patients suffering from gout stand on a torpedo fish as a cure. The electricity from the fish would numb the patient's feet and legs, thereby preventing pain. Also, in Britain during the 18th century, it cost gout patients two shillings and sixpence to be treated by a "torporific fish."

The electric eel is not an eel at all but a close cousin to the carp and catfish. Living in the murky waters of South America, mostly the Amazon Basin, scientists have found it difficult to study this fish in its own habitat and to capture it for aquarium study, therefore, only recently have some of its unique characteristics been revealed. The electric eel is probably the only fish that can swim forward and backward with equal speed and although born with eye sight, becomes totally blind when it reaches maturity. It grows to a length of from four to 12 feet and can weigh over 50 lbs. The electric eel does have gills, but if forced to remain underwater for ten minutes or more it will drown. It must come to the surface about 180 times a day to breathe air. It finds its food by using a nature-made radar device in its head and then it shocks its prey by discharging electricity from its tail. Anyone who touches an electric eel is in for a shock, for they continuously emit small voltages up to 400 times per second and when disturbed or excited, are capable of discharging 600 volts of electricity, more than enough to kill a man. At the 1939 New York World's Fair, electric eels were used to send telegraph messages and run electric trains. Only two other fish are capable of giving electric shocks, the star-gazer, mostly found in the South Atlantic, and the electric catfish of Africa's Nile River. The star-gazer has eyes on the top of its head and therefore can completely bury itself in a sandy bottom and still watch for small fish swimming by. When a fish comes near, it emits a shock wave which paralyzes the fish and then the star-gazer sucks it in.

Another fish that covers itself with sand and usually waits for an unknowing fish to come along is the angler fish, also known as the goosefish. It is by far one of the ugliest, most repulsive fish in the sea with a mouth almost a big as its body. The body of the goosefish is flat and ray-like. Instead of using electricity to catch fish, it has a worm-like appendage that dangles from its forehead and when a fish snaps at this appendage, the goosefish merely yawns and the fish is gobbled up. The goosefish sometimes walks along the bottom on ventral fins that look like human hands and pectoral fins that resemble human arms. It comes to the surface now and then to catch a duck or gull which it swallows whole. In 1943, two boys who were fishing in Massachusetts Bay saw a goosefish swallow a duck that had been resting on the water. The boys then managed to hook the goosefish and cut it open to find the duck still alive inside. They nursed the duck back to health and kept it for a pet for the rest of its natural life. Also in Massachusetts at Nantasket Beach, ten year old Robert O'Neil of Dorchester poked at a big, 20 lb. fish he saw lying in the shallows. The goosefish immediately jumped out of the water and grabbed Robert's arm. A nearby lifeguard tried to make the fish let go by hitting it with a shovel. The goosefish then released Robert's arm and bit into the shovel. Robert's arm had

15 deep punctures and several lacerations. Goosefish have also been known to bite divers, but it is always the female of the species that does the biting. The male goosefish which is much smaller than its mate, attaches itself to the female early in life and becomes a parasite and serves only as a reproductive organ. The female, however, can weigh 75 lbs. or more and as ugly as she is, is marketed as food in America, parts of Europe and Japan.

Another smaller cousin of the goosefish is the batfish, which looks like a ray, but has two paddle-like pectoral fins that resemble a flying bat. Actually the batfish is an awkward swimmer, so it usually walks along the ocean floor. It has also been seen walking along the beach out of water, but this is probably because the batfish is so slow it finds itself high and dry when the tide goes out. When this happens it slowly walks back into the water again. The batfish, which never grows larger than one foot, has a natural fishing rod like the goosefish. When it's hungry, a worm-like rod protrudes from its head to attract little fish.

The leopard-ray, distinquished cousin of the mantaray and stingray, and distant cousin of the shark, is a harmless, even friendly fish.
Photo by Paul Tzimoulis

Another member of the angler family is the sargassum fish which never grows to more than six inches and lives in the Atlantic's floating weed beds. As tiny as it is, the sargassum fish is just as aggressive as its big cousin the goose-fish. It will attack fish twice its size and try to swallow them whole in its large mouth. It also has hand-like pectoral fins and often climbs out of the water and up and down the floating sargassum weed looking for insects. Recently a group of scientists collected 25 sargassum fish to study them under controlled conditions. After being in an aquarium for less than two hours, scientists found only one fat sargassum fish left and it was walking along the top of the glass case looking for something more to eat.

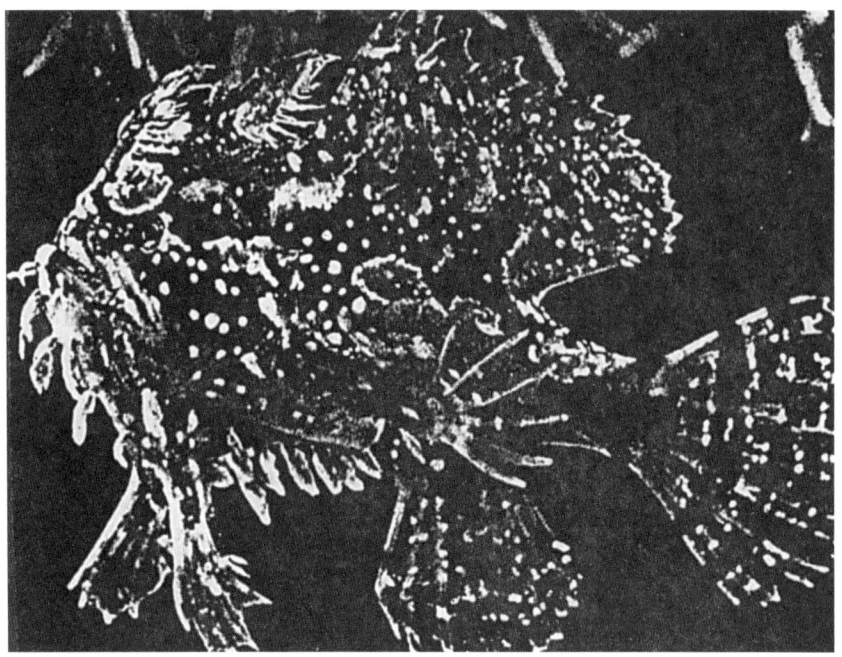

The six inch sargassum fish, probably the toughest fish in the sea, can also live out of water.

There are more than one species of fish that can walk on land and the most prominent is the six inch blenny, found in tropical waters just about everywhere in the world. Blennies leave the water voluntarily at low tide and spend almost as much time skipping along the rocky beach as they do underwater. They walk on their ventral fins and must periodically duck their heads into tidal pools to wash water over their gills. Their gill sacks carry a water supply and when they are dried up, the blenny must return to the sea. Blennies kept in aquariums will jump out of their tanks twice a day and remain out of water for about five or six hours, always at tow tide, even though they can't see the ocean and may be miles away from it. A ferocious member of the blenny family is the saber-toothed blenny that has two fangs in its lower lip and attacks fish three to four times its size by first biting out their eyes. Another larger family member found in the North Atlantic and Pacific is the wolf fish or wolf eel. These creatures have fierce looking wolf-like faces and teeth to match, which they will use without hesitation. However, Pacific coast scientists say that wolf eels in captivity become fairly tame. These overgrown blennies can grow to eight feet and weigh 40 or more pounds. They live in cold water and can be found in shallow water or at depths up to 600 feet. They are also known as "the catfish of the sea."

Fresh water catfish, although sleepy, slow-moving bottom creatures, have been known to give a human a good bite and the European variety will pluck a bird from the surface waters and drag it under for dinner. Catfish also come in many sizes, from the three inch home aquarium size to the 200 lb. variety, found in large lakes and rivers. Fisherman Dick Tinnel caught a 47 lb. catfish in Lake Texoma, Oklahoma in 1958, but the record catch was off St. Louis in 1878 when a 150 lb. catfish, measuring five feet, was taken from the Mississippi. There are catfish called "manguruyus" living in the Amazon River that come 12 feet in length and have been known to swallow a native now and then. European catfish have also been known to reach a length of 12 feet and some of these larger whiskered cats have spines in their dorsal fins that carry a mild poison.

There is a type of South American catfish, called a lungfish, that lives in and out of fresh water, feeding on large fish, lizards and small animals. When rivers dry up these lungfish often wrap themselves up in a ball of mud and live without water for months until the rains return to fill up the rivers. Explorer Hyatt Verrill once reported that natives living along the jungle rivers complained that lungfish were attacking their chickens. In one village where the river dried up, lungfish invaded hen houses and were seen carrying off chickens in their mouths.

A similar situation recently existed in Florida and in 1969, Florida's Director of Fisheries, John Woods, announced that walking catfish were attacking small animals and depleting fish supplies in the northern part of the state and that the catfish were migrating south. "We're giving up," Woods reported. "The catfish invaders are not only here to stay but are hiking into new territories. It's impossible to get rid of them." The walking catfish crawl on their fins from pond to pond and can remain out of water for over 12 hours breathing air. During that time they can travel approximately six miles.

There is a fish called a mudskipper that can travel over land faster than man. It comes out of the Pacific Ocean every day at low tide and runs quickly over the mud on its pectoral fins. The West Coast grumion also comes ashore for a brief time to bury eggs in the sand, but then she quickly returns to the sea. In India, China and Africa there are two types of fresh water perch that obtain their food by coming out of the water and climbing trees for insects. These eight inch perch live out of water for long periods of time breathing air to survive rather than pumping water through their gills for oxygen. Some scientists believe that soon these fish will reach a stage in evolution that they will not wish to return to the sea and will live their lives in the trees.

The ugly eel-like lamprey fish also leaves the water and climbs over rocks by using its suckling mouth to move from one spot to another. The name lamprey means "rock sucker" and the lamprey's mouth, which never closes, secretes a chemical called lampetrin that rots fish flesh on contact. The lamprey attaches its strong mouth to a fish, then its row of jagged teeth located on the tongue, cuts through the fish into its intestines. Lampreys can live in fresh water as well as salt and can grow to a size of three feet. They fear nothing and will attack anything, including a whale. Their cousin the slime eel, also called hagfish, attaches itself to other fish and eats its way inside until the entire fish is consumed. They also go through life with their mouths open and have toothed tongues. They prefer to hunt in deep water up to 300 feet and because they are shaped like a sausage, without fins, they move very slowly in the water and, to add to their problems, they are totally blind. The slender gar-pike doesn't have teeth in its mouth but its throat is lined with canines and its mouth is like a bird's beak. Although the gar-pike is not as aggressive as the lamprey and hagfish it will attack without hesitation, using its beak as a spear. Its body is shaped like a barracuda but some have mistaken it for an eel. An added distinction of the gar-pike is that it is probably the only fish that has green colored bones.

Another beaked fish that can on occasion be dangerous to man is the slender, 12 inch long needlefish. Swiftly skimming over the surface waters, needlefish have accidentally imbedded their long noses into human flesh. Two Mexican fisherman recently died when they were stabbed in the throat by needlefish, and fishermen and bathers have been seriously wounded by needlefish off the Florida coast. A larger member of the needlefish family is the houndfish, which can grow to a length of five feet and can strike another fish or a human with the impact of a javelin. The tiny half-beak fish is also a relative and although it is missing the long upper jaw, it successfully impales fish on its sharp lower jaw.

Other beaked fish include such giants as marlin, sailfish, swordfish and sawfish and all are among the fastest fish in the world. There are three species of marlin that vary in size from 100 lbs. to 1,000 lbs. They use their sharp bills to jab other fish and have been known to stab boats, as was the case in 1956, when a blue marlin attacked the Marine Research Vessel GERDA. The blue marlin and the swordfish can travel up to 60 miles per hour in the water and like the 100 lb. sailfish, can leap 40 to 50 feet out of water. The sailfish is probably the fastest fish in the world and can swim at speeds up to 70 miles per hour. The swordfish, with a beak that can measure five feet in length, will also attack ships and has imbedded its bill up to two feet through solid wood. It has also been responsible for sinking a few ships. Even unprovoked swordfish have charged ships for no apparent reason. One attacked the fishing vessel PUBNICO PAL off Nova Scotia and its beak punctured a one foot hole in the ship's planking. A few years ago, a 200 lb. broadbill swordfish tried to stab through the steel hull of the research submarine ALVIN at Blake's Plateau in the Atlantic. ALVIN's hull was only scratched and the stunned swordfish was brought to the surface and eaten.

While fishing with a new plastic line some 100 miles off the Bermuda Islands, the crew of an American research vessel hauled in an 11 foot swordfish. The fish wasn't hooked but its beak was stuck in the two inch thick plastic. There were holes in the plastic line indicating that the swordfish had attacked it many times before it got stuck. Two Baltic Sea fishermen reported that in June, 1970, they spent five hours fighting a swordfish that got trapped in their fishing nets. "It attacked our boat many times," reported the Polish fishermen, "and our boat was leaking badly when we finally hauled it aboard." The biggest swordfish ever caught by commercial fishermen weighed 1,100 lbs. and was 16 feet long. The biggest catch by a sports fisherman was when Louis Marron snagged a 1,182 pounder off the coast of Chile. A 266 lb. swordfish caught recently by a sports fisherman at Cuttyhunk, Massachusetts, had a 125 lb. blue shark impaled on its beak.

The sawfish, which is actually a member of the ray family, can live in fresh water as well as salt. It has attacked boats and there are a few cases where it has ascended rivers and attacked bathers, although, like other members of the ray family, it will not strike out unless provoked. Its hard, flat saw protruding from its head, can have up to 68 teeth, 34 on each side, which it uses to cut up its food before eating. A sawfish will swim into a school of fish and whip its head back and forth, wounding many in the school. Sawfish can measure 20 feet from saw-tip to tail and can weigh up to 1,300 lbs. They are also speedy underwater swimmers.

There is also a long snouted fresh water fish found in the rivers of Central United States and in parts of China. It is called the paddlefish, or the flatbill, or the shovel-nosed catfish. The Chinese paddlefish can weigh almost 1,000 lbs. and measure 20 feet in length. The biggest American paddlefish ever caught was taken from Reelfoot Lake, Tennessee. It was five feet long and weighed 184 lbs. The ugly and toothless paddlefish lives on plankton and scientists believe it finds food with a natural sensing device located in its long flat beak. The paddlefish, like the shark, has no bones and fishermen of the Mississippi and Missouri Rivers consider it a great game fish and a good tasting one as

The giant 400-pound grouper, also known as sea bass, sea cod, warsaws, cherna, and jewfish. It is usually friendly, but its size makes it fearsome. It also tastes good and can feed a big family–it's a great prize for fishermen and spearfishermen.
Photo courtesy of Folco Quilici

well. The eggs of the female paddlefish are used to make caviar. The paddlefish, like all the other long nosed fish, is a fast swimmer.

There has always been controversy among sports fishermen as to which species of fish can swim the fastest, but very few fish have been "clocked" with electronic equipment. Most speed timings have been inaccurate estimates made by fishermen or yachtsmen. The barracuda however, was electrically timed at speeds up to 27 miles per hour and the wahoo was clocked off Florida swimming at 40 miles per hour. Tuna can swim steadily at nine miles per hour without stopping, which means a 15 year old tuna has probably traveled about one million miles. At top speed, tuna can swim at 60 miles per hour. Most fish travel at top speed an average of ten times their body length per second and most fish can jump out of water by exerting a thrust of four times their weight. Flying fish can jump to heights 50 feet above the surface water and can glide over the water at 35 miles per hour for distances of 400 yards. The king mackerel can jump up to 30 feet out of water. It does so by taking water into its mouth and squirting it through its gills. The backward force of the water propels the fish into the air. Salmon can jump eight feet and up to 20 feet when leaping waterfalls. One versatile fish called the flying gurnard can jump up to 20 feet out of water, can skim over the surface at 30 miles per hour, swim at a speed of 35 miles per hour and can also walk on land.

Probably the most remarkably determined fish is the salmon. It is born and grows up in fresh water, leaves its stream and goes to sea for two or more years, then returns to its fresh water home to spawn and die. While living in the sea where food is more abundant, salmon gain as much as one pound a month in body weight and travel as far as 1,500 miles away from the mouth of the river they were born in. Yet they return, not only to their river, but to the very brook or pond of their birth. Some Alaskan salmon must journey inland for over 2,000 miles, climbing waterfalls and fighting swift currents to get back to the brook of their birth. It takes some European salmon over one year to make the fresh water trip, but when the going isn't too tough, they can travel at a rate of 50 miles a day.

One tagged two-year-old salmon left the Prairie Creek Fish Hatchery, California, in 1964. It returned from the sea to the hatchery five years later. To make the long journey back to what this salmon considered home, it first swam two creeks and through a culvert under Highway 101. It then squeezed through a four inch drainpipe, jumped through a pipe located three feet above the drainpipe and leaped over a two-foot high wire fence. It then had the choice of five pipes to swim through, four of which were blocked up at the opposite end. The salmon chose the correct pipe and swam into the hatchery tank.

When salmon return to fresh water, no matter how long or difficult the journey home, they never eat a morsel of food during the trip. Many of them loose up to 49% of their body weight before they reach their destination. Most salmon die after they return home and spawn, but some Atlantic salmon live through it, return to the sea and come back three or four more times in their lifetime to spawn. Many salmon live seven years in the sea before they return to fresh water, but all pink salmon spend no more than two years in salt water before returning to fresh. The steelhead trout, like its salmon cousins, migrates to the sea and returns to fresh water a few years later to spawn, but it usually survives the spawn. It will also strike at a fisherman's flyrod during the journey back home, something that 95% of the salmon won't do. Hungry trout also feed on salmon eggs and this is one reason why only one fish out of 3,000 eggs laid by female salmon survives. Hatcheries have, of course, increased salmon survival rates, but recently at the Avon and Dorset River Hatchery, England, something went wrong. The British scientists announced that even though artificial insemination was used to spawn salmon, "that wasn't the reason for the strange results." They believed that the monsters they created were probably due to "the lateness of the spawning date in January." Whatever the reason, the result was 20,000 two-headed salmon. The British scientists managed to calm the fearful Avon River fishermen by reporting that all the deformed salmon died within one month of hatching.

There are other fish, including striped bass and alewives, that leave salt water to spawn in fresh, and once their duties are completed, will return to the sea. Like salmon, striped bass give up feeding when they enter fresh water and although evidence is not complete, many alewives, like salmon, return to the stream of their birth to spawn. The University of Rhode Island is presently experimenting with alewives in an effort to discover how and why they seek their birth places after spending years in the sea. Thus far it is theorized that alewives can distinguish one river or stream from another by smell and are able to sniff out the assortment of minerals that make up their home stream. Alewives, also known as buckeyes and river herring, are in demand on America's East Coast but have become a nuisance in the Great Lakes, especially in Lake Michigan, where every three to four years, dead alewives numbering in the billions wash ashore after spawning. It is estimated that this natural kill in Lake Michigan costs $100 million in cleanup costs and loss of tourist trade.

An eight-foot moray attacks a diver while he attempts to spear it–the diver won.
Photo by Paul Tzimoulis.

Even with salmon and trout feeding on alewives and fishermen catching them by the thousands every year, the alewives of the Mid-West are experiencing a population explosion.

Eels reverse the salmon, trout and alewives spawning procedure. Instead of venturing from fresh water to salt and back again, all common "fresh water" eels are born in salt water. When they are hatched they swim from their South Atlantic birthplace to the rivers and streams of Europe and America. This is a one year journey for the American eels and a three year trip for the European species. Of the 120 or so species of eels that make their home in fresh water, some live as long as 50 years and grow to a size of four to seven feet. When it's time to spawn and die, they head for saltwater and the Sargasso Sea, their place of birth. The female of the common eel family is very prolific, laying up to ten million eggs. The offspring, even those found in land-locked bodies of water, are products of the Sargasso Sea. These young eels reach ponds and lakes far inland by slithering over wetlands and damp eel grass at night.

A new species of eel was discovered some thirty years ago in the Gulf of Akuba, Jordan, called "garden eels." These tiny creatures live on the sea bot-

A Green Moray eel with jaws agape. The eel was photographed in a rock crevice off La Paz, Mexico.

Photo by Paul Tzimoulis

tom with their heads and most of their upper body sticking out of sand holes. Row upon row of them can be seen swaying in the current, like fields of tall grass blowing in the wind. Garden eels direct their heads toward the currents to catch small fish and other morsels that drift by. When a large fish or diver approaches them, they duck their heads back into the sand holes. The eels dig these holes with their tails. Contained in their tails is a glue-like substance that allows them to secure themselves to the sea bottom. Another rare salt water eel, larger in size than the garden eel and living only a few miles down the coast in the Red Sea, is the white sea eel. It is a milky white color, can grow to a size of almost three feet and is found only in the southern waters of the Red Sea.

The two most common saltwater eels are the conger and the moray, both ugly creatures with powerful teeth that won't hesitate to bite when provoked. They also have the nasty habit of never letting go once they sink their teeth into something. The conger and the moray can be dangerous out of water too. They can live for hours out of water on moisture which is stored up in their gills. A South Seas fisherman in 1994 was forced to abandon his boat when a four-foot moray got loose on deck and he wasn't able to return until three hours later. I have seen captured congers squirm around on deck snapping at everything in sight with their three rows of chunky teeth. Once, as a boy, I stuck a block of wood into a captured conger's mouth and it clamped down its jaws. When the eel died about two hours later, I still couldn't ply the wood from the conger's mouth. Also, the blood of these sea dragons is highly toxic and if but a teaspoon full were injected into a man, he would die instantly.

Conger eels live in cold waters, mostly in the North Atlantic and one was captured there weighing 85 lbs. and measuring nine feet in length. The average size of a conger is two to three feet. In 1778, English writer C. Gould reported that a Major Wolf, swimming in a bay near Wicklow, England, was chased in the water by a large eel with a "huge, bulldog head." The eel attacked the Major, but he was able to scramble ashore. Gould also tells us that a Wicklow farmer named Burbridge had a similar experience at the same spot in the early 1700s. Burbridge described the creature that came after him as "a giant conger, some 20 feet long." In 1781, the body of a swimmer was found off the Yorkshire coast and had wounds that were definitely the marks of conger teeth.

Morays, dwelling in the coral caves of tropical waters, can measure eight feet and weigh 50 lbs. An American skin-diver named Nick Fleeman recently speared and captured a moray off Okinawa that weighed 45 lbs. Like the conger, the moray prowls at night and remains in its cave with just its head poking out during daylight hours. The green moray is the most common of the family and its smaller cousin, the speckled moray, is the rarer breed. Both have a evil grin and sharp, fang-like teeth and their heads move too and fro as they breathe in water through their necks, giving them the appearance of a cobra being charmed by some silent flute. In an effort to prove that all fish are friendly if you treat them right, divers of Florida and California have been swimming down to moray caves and hand-feeding them shrimp and other tasty treats. Thus far, the morays have accepted the gifts of food without taking off a diver's finger or hand. Divers even pat the morays' heads while hand feeding them, but this is far from proof that the moray can always be soothed into docility by man.

There is a documented case where a fresh water eel actually saved an entire community. The people of Durham, Connecticut, had constructed the first water supply for public use in America, completed on February 22, 1798. The water was piped into the town from a spring that was fed by the Coginchaug River. The narrow pipes were first made of wood and in 1828, converted to lead pipes some two inches in diameter, but it wasn't too many years before they silted up and only a dribble of water flowed into town. The summers are hot in Connecticut and the townsfolk couldn't quench their thirst. Using good old Yankee ingenuity, the town fathers procured a three-foot eel from the river and inserted it into the pipe at the upper end. It took six hours for the eel to swim through, but when it wiggled out at the other end, all the clogging sediment came with it and the people of Durham had water again.

Divers today disagree as to whether or not the sluggish, bottom dwelling grouper is a dangerous marine animal or one of the friendliest fish in the sea. In the book "Our World Underwater," author Bill Stephens mentions two authenticated cases where divers were swallowed by groupers and although both escaped, one man was severely injured. There are underwater movies available showing groupers frolicking with divers and nestling up to them like kittens hugging your legs when you approach the refrigerator. Groupers, also called sea-bass, sea-cod, jewfish and warsaws, can grow to a length of ten feet and weigh over 600 lbs. and they are one of the largest mouthed fish in the sea. Groupers don't eat their food, they just open their mouths and breathe it in. When a grouper lowers its jaw it sets up a flow of water toward its mouth and anything caught in this current is taken into its stomach. In Tahiti, groupers are called "hapuu" and are greatly feared. There are stories in the islands of natives being swallowed whole by hapuu, yet skin-divers visiting these waters say that hapuu are very friendly and make excellent undersea pets. In Nassau there is a grouper named Harry that is a permanent inhabitant of the local marina. Harry greets tourists, performs tricks and sticks out his fin to shake hands with every skin-diver that passes by, but when Harry opens his mouth, even if it's just to yawn, divers keep their distance, for as one visiting diver said, "The suction is enough to find your foot in Harry's mouth." Also, the hard gill covers of groupers is enough to crush a diver's ribs and, "Harry loves to give you a little brush with his body when you pass by." Harry, like most groupers, is just a happy-go-lucky giant that doesn't know his own strength.

Like the underside of ray-fish, the sturgeon has a toothless mouth for sucking food off the bottom, and two sets of barbells to recognize its favorite food by touch.

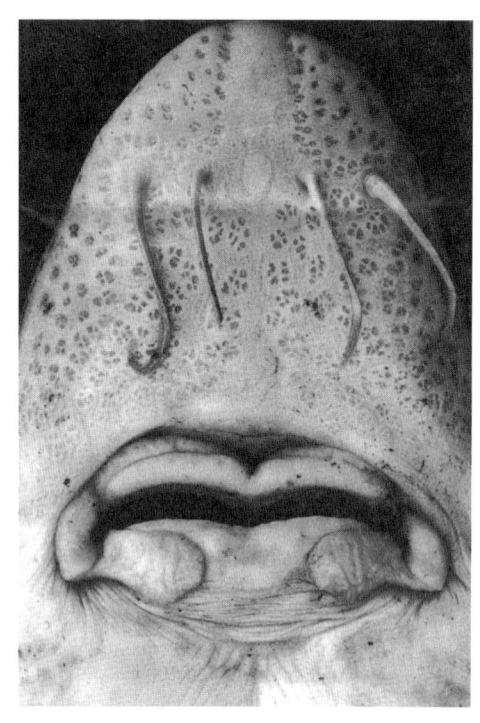

The gaping jaws and needle-like teeth of the goosefish. It swallows birds and other fish whole.
Photos by Paul Tzimoulis.

Groupers also have the ability to change the color of their skin at will, to blend in with the surroundings. If their home happens to be near grey colored rocks, their skin is grey and if they are swimming around a sandy bottom, their skin color is light brown. Most of the grouper family, like the yellow-finned grouper, is colored a dark brown but when alarmed, it changes color immediately to blend with its hiding place.

There are many species of fish that can change color tones like a chameleon and can often change skin patterns. Scientists believe for the most part that fish do not have control over the ability, but that it is triggered by nerves or by pituitary hormones. Eyesight does play a part, for experiments with a one-eyed trout showed that when placed in different colored environments, only one side of the fish would change color to match the surroundings. A flounder, placed in a tank with a checkerboard bottom pattern, tried to match the squares and although it didn't completely succeed, the top skin pattern and pigment did come fairly close to the checkerboard. Fish like cunner or chaugies that live in and around a rocky bottom will become an orange-red color if they decide to make their home in a rusty old shipwreck. The filefish that stands up vertically on the bottom when frightened, also changes color tone to match the bottom. When swimming head down in eel-grass it looks like another blade of grass. Also, when the gout fish turns upside down it automatically changes color. The coral-cad is another that changes color to blend with its dwelling. The stone fish will cover itself with green algae if necessary to camouflage itself for although it too can change skin tone, it can't make the color green so it allows the algae to grow on its back. Some fish can change into eight or more different colors and patterns to match their mood or surroundings and nearly all fish carry the colors of the waters they swim in. Bottom fish are usually brown, grey or greenish to match the immediate area in which they live and open sea fish have blue or green backs, depending on the color of the surface waters. If the waters below are silvery, their bellies are white and if the depths are muddy, their stomachs are often brown. There are of course exceptions such as the yellow butterfly fish and the rainbow and clown fishes that are made up of bright, colorful markings and surprisingly, there are not two rainbow fish in the sea that have the same markings. There is the glass prawn that is transparent and through its glass-like skin you can see its insides working. The colorful jewelfish stands out like a painter's palette on the coral bottom, yet it moves so fast that it is almost impossible to capture. In fact, divers should know that aquariumists will pay $50.00 if you can bring back a live jewelfish for their tanks. Another striking tropical fish is the corb fish which is colored bronze and has a pearly white gem-like concretion growing from its forehead. The gem is used in many countries to make necklaces. There is also the bright orange garibaldi or ocean goldfish that stands out like a Christmas tree bulb on the greenish bottom. Being so bright, the garibaldi is easy prey to bigger fish and skin-divers, but in California it is protected from skin-divers because it is the official state fish. However, most other fish and spearfishermen don't bother garibaldis, for they taste awful.

One fish that did a reverse on mother nature is the African catfish. Its belly is brown and its back is a musty white. If it swam like most fish, the white back would attract thousands of bigger fish to gobble it up, but the African catfish swims upside down and therefore only its brown belly is exposed to other fish. Its belly blends in with the muddy surroundings. The trumpetfish and the seahorse, like the pipe fish, swim vertically and the green seahorse not only blends with undersea vegetation, but uses its tail to wrap around the vegetation to secure it to the bottom. Another fish that stands on its head is the stickleback but it does so only to frighten off other fish when it's protecting a nest of eggs.

The male stickleback is a devoted father and husband, up to a point. He builds a nest for his mate weaving together pieces of undersea vegetation, much like a bird builds its nest out of straw and twigs. The female then lays her eggs in the nest and he fertilizes them. He then kicks out the female and he guards the nest until the eggs hatch. After that the little sticklebacks are on their own. Papa stickleback is a great dad as long as the water temperature around the nest doesn't cool down. For some unknown reason, if the water around him cools, his temper rises and he attacks every member of his family. Even more dedicated is the little sarcastic-fringehead of the Pacific. The male of this species also guards the female's eggs by hiding them inside some empty seashell. He goes without food while he tends the nursery and he's so exhausted by the time the babies go off to school that he can hardly move and is usually gobbled up by some passing fish. The male fish that really goes to extremes as the time for birth for his offspring approaches is the seahorse. A few weeks before he becomes a parent, the female seahorse deposits her eggs in his nature-made kangaroo-like stomach pouch. Within the pouch, the male fertilizes the eggs and soon the fully formed seacolts emerge, usually 20 to 25 of them. At this point the mother attaches herself to a nearby piece of vegetation and seemingly suffers the pangs of childbirth by going through all kinds of contortions. The male pipefish, cousin to the seahorse, also fertilizes the female's eggs in its stomach pouch and incubates the eggs for up to 20 days until they're ready to hatch and swim off on their own.

The male South American catfish is also an overly devoted father. After his mate has laid her eggs, which are as big as marbles, he sucks them up into his mouth and carries them around in his mouth for days until they hatch. He keeps the baby catfish inside his locked jaws until they are ready to venture into the cruel sea. Even when the young ones are off fending for themselves during the day, they return to dad's mouth at night until they just can't fit anymore. During this time, the usually carnivorous male catfish doesn't eat a thing.

One large catfish netted by fishermen in Peru had over 50 eggs in its mouth when captured.

The male Betta fish, also known as the Siamese fighting fish, blows bubbles from its mouth while the female is giving birth. The baby Bettas are then pushed into the bubbles by their father and this becomes their protective home until they are mature enough to swim away and fend for themselves. It's what ichthyologists call a "bubble birth." The male and female blenny not only take turns watching over the eggs, but when the youngsters emerge, each parent sucks them one at a time into their mouths and spits them out into the sea to start them on their way. If per chance a recently hatched blenny isn't washed in either parent's mouth, it will not survive for more than an hour or so.

Fish eggs cannot hatch until fertilized by the male sperm and in most cases the eggs are deposited by the female and then fertilized by the male. The black seabass in fact builds a nest of stones on the sea floor before he has found a mate. He then waits in his nest until a ripe one comes along. Sometimes, before the spawning season is over, he will have invited four or five females into his nest. After she lays her eggs, the female leaves and the male bass is often left with 10,000 or more eggs to watch over for a period of two weeks. The little male annual fish, sometimes called killifish, waits impatiently for the female to lay her eggs in some little pond or rain puddle. He then fertilizes the eggs and cares for them, but the puddle soon dries up and the parents die. During the next rain, the eggs hatch and the cycle continues, with all killifish being born, spawning and dying within a year.

There are a few species of fish, like land animals, that suffer the pangs and pains of childbirth. One is the eelpout that hatches her eggs inside her body after they have been fertilized by the male. She then swims around for four months burdened with up to 300 little eelpouts wiggling inside her stomach. The male molly also fertilizes eggs while they are inside the female and the youngsters are born fully formed. As any aquarium owner knows, starting with just a male and female molly today could mean a full tank of mollies tomorrow. The male molly however, will sometimes eat many of his offspring.

A seemingly painful pregnancy is suffered by the female skate and stingray, whose eggs are square and have little horns at each of four corners. She lays 10 to 20 of these three-inch long, hard shelled eggs at one sitting and if per chance she is hooked by a fisherman while carrying these egg sacs she will automatically give birth. Although her eggs hardly ever wash ashore, in the 18th century when they were found on the beaches, some people thought they were mermaid's purses. Maybe the female codfish has it tougher than the stingray, for she lays up to eight million eggs a year, and one 54 lb. ling cod caught by fishermen carried over 28,000,000 eggs. Only about one percent of a cod's offspring reaches maturity but if all codfish that were born managed to live, there would be no room in the Atlantic Ocean for any other fish within eight years.

Some fish eggs contain an oil that keeps them afloat on the surface waters. Others, like herring eggs, are coated with a sticky substance that permanently glues them to any object they contact until they are ready to hatch. A few years ago an oil tanker from Seattle, Washington, entered Los Angeles Harbor with billions of Pacific herring eggs attached to her hull. The captain of the tanker reported that, "the sticky eggs reduced the speed of the ship by nearly two knots per hour." The eggs were all dead when they reached Los Angeles and the California Department of Fish and Game reported that the mass death was due to the changing water temperatures between Washington and California.

During the mating season, usually in the Spring, many species of fish turn bright colors. The cuckoo wrasse for example, changes from a green to a brilliant blue and gold as he searches out a suitable mate. The male dragonet fish takes on a bright multi-colored coat and dances in front of the females until one of them is impressed. The two of them then swim off together toward the surface as she lays her eggs and he fertilizes them. The male and female wrasse also perform a dancing ceremony while mating. They stand upright over their nest and sway back and forth facing each other and as their bodies shiver in typical modern dancing fashion, they open and close their mouths and wave their pectoral fins. Divers have also witnessed groupers weighing up to 70 lbs. standing upright on the ocean floor and spinning around on their tails in a ritual ballet. No one really knows why these hefty creatures dance together, but some ichthyologists believe it is a mating ceremony.

There are also sexy little creatures called gourmis in the Indian Ocean that spend part of every day kissing each other. Although this amorous mouth to mouth contact was once thought to be part of a mating ritual, it is actually a game of tug-of-war. The gourmis grasp each other by the mouth and push backwards in an effort to test their strength. Two truly love-sick fish are the mullet and bass and a fisherman can easily catch the male of these species during the mating season if he catches the female first. Allowing the female to dance on the end of the line will bring forth the lustful male, who has been known to follow his mate anywhere, even onto a dry beach.

There are a few species of fish, including groupers, hamlets and an eel called *"monopterus albus"* that are born one sex and die another. Some groupers are born female but change to male about ten years later and remain male for the remaining two-thirds of their life. The monopterus albus is born female and becomes male within a few years. Both male and female sex organs are contained within the hamlet fish and it too starts out as a female and gradually becomes a male. The gilt-head fish also leads a confusing sex life. Its male organs mature first so that at age two, it's a male, but one year later it becomes female. There is a Pacific Ocean seaworm that starts life as a male and with age becomes a female, but when it is hungry it changes back to a male. If it ever gets cut in half, both halves become whole worms and are a different sex than the original whole worm. It is also interesting to note that sexual relations between fish of different species are possible and such relations have resulted in interesting and sometimes scientifically and commercially beneficial offspring. Most of these mongrels however, don't live very long, or are unable to create offspring of their own.

Most fish don't have long lives and few species reach the ripe old age of 20. In fact, fish like the goby and killifish live only one year. Most scientists now believe that when a fish stops growing, deterioration sets in and the fish quickly dies. The age of a fish can be determined by the markings on its scales. Every dark ring on a fish scale represents one year. Some ichthyologists, instead of killing a fish to count the dark rings on its scales, will cut off its scales, for the fish will grow back new scales within a few weeks. Another way to determine the age and growth of fish is by counting the ridges on its otoliths, or ear stones. Round, bone-like otoliths are part of the fish's equilibrium mechanism. They were once carried by superstitious seamen to ward off evil spirits and some people who have found them on the beaches have mistaken them for pearls. Today, some people collect them for scientific purposes and some, like seashell collectors, just for the fun of it. One collector, Don Frizzell of Missouri, has thousands of otoliths from over 800 species of fish.

Through the above mentioned methods it has been determined that a codfish can live to age 25 and the herring lives to be about 23 years old. Groupers in captivity have lived to be 30 and probably live longer in the sea. Even the little minnow can reach age 40 and carps can survive to age 49. It has often been said by old timers that catfish can live to be 100, but the oldest one ever captured was only 61 years old. As I mentioned earlier, eels can live to age 60, but the oldest fish ever captured was recently netted in a Canadian lake. It was a 215 lb. sturgeon that had lived 152 years. The Russians have reported that they have caught sturgeons in the Caspian Sea that were over 200 years old.

Sturgeons can grow to 16 feet in length and can weigh over a ton, but they don't reach sexual maturity until they are 10 to 15 years old. A mature female can lay one million eggs at one sitting and it's from these eggs that caviar is produced. A large female sturgeon can provide 300 lbs. of caviar. When sturgeons were more plentiful in America, before pollution, many coastal restaurants served caviar sandwiches as a regular bill of fare. Russian caviar is still a favorite throughout the world, presently selling at $40.00 to $60.00 per pound. In 1941, to keep their caviar and sturgeon "red meat" business alive, the Russians imported 65,000 seaworms to the Caspian Sea to feed their hungry sturgeons.

Sturgeons love to eat and they continuously scour the bottom, their toothless mouths sucking in the food like a vacuum cleaner. They also have barbells growing from their chins to search out eatables, but their eyes are but slits and they can't see very well. Sturgeons are often confused with surgeons, or doctor fish, that have two sharp curved scales at the base of their tail that can wound another fish or human with a thin, scalpel-like cut. Sturgeons however, are actually prehistoric fish that, unlike most other ancient animals are defenseless, but have survived for over 300 million years. In 1922, Russia reported that fishermen in the Volga Basin caught a sturgeon weighing 2,700 lbs. and also in the Volga in 1892, one was captured that weighed 3,000 lbs.

There aren't many fish that come bigger than the sturgeon, except maybe mantas that have been caught weighing over 3,500 lbs. and a sunfish that was captured in the Pacific measuring only eight feet, but weighing 3,102 lbs. Blue and black marlins can weigh 2,000 lbs. and California seabass can weigh 800 lbs. Groupers can weigh over 600 lbs. and one was recently beached off the Texas Gulf Coast weighing 539 lbs. The biggest Atlantic salmon was caught in 1901 off the coast of Scotland. It weighed 104 lbs. and the world record tuna was snagged by a sports fisherman at St. Ann's Bay, Cape Breton in 1968. It weighed 977 lbs. Although swordfish can weigh 2,000 lbs., a six month old swordfish is less than 1/2 inch long and hardly weighs an ounce, yet a trout of the same age is twice as long and weighs up to three times as much.

South African Ichtheologist, J.C. Smith, examines the prehistoric coelacanth, brought to the surface at Madagascar in 1952.

The size of the body of water in which a fish lives, plus its diet, determines and controls its size. Blue fish of the Atlantic for example, eat twice their own weight every day, but if placed in a smaller body of water with less to eat, blue fish wouldn't grow to half their normal size. In the Pacific Ocean, between Panama and Mexico, fish grow to an unusually large size and for some unknown reason, they live longer and are more immune to diseases than their counterparts living in other areas. Apparently the waters off Panama contain ingredients that greatly enhance the growth and strength of fish, but scientists are still baffled as to how and why.

Even more baffling to marine scientists was the appearance of a coelacanth in 1938. The existence of this large, crusty-skinned fish was as startling a discovery as finding a live dinosaur, for the coelacanth was thought to be extinct for at least 60 million years. Fossils of these fish had previously been found imbedded in rock dating back 350 million years. The live 127 lb., five-foot fossil dredged from 300 feet off South Africa, is still considered one of the greatest discoveries of the twentieth century. This fish had a large head with canine teeth, a broad tail and fins shaped somewhat like human legs. Many scientists believe the coelacanth is the "missing link" between man and fish and was intimately related to the first animal that walked on land. In 1952, a second live coelacanth was fished up at Comoro Island, Madagascar, from a depth of 600 feet and since then, about 40 others have been captured in the Indian Ocean off Comoro Island. It was recently revealed that these islanders have been fishing for coelacanths for years at depths of 300 to 2,000 feet and that they were sold on the island as food. In 1965, French scuba diver Jacques Stevens went to Comoro Island and photographed a live coelacanth at night, swimming at a depth of 150 feet. He reported that although this prehistoric fish looks dangerous, it is not aggressive. Its eyes glow in the dark and its chunky tail acts as a keel, directing its movements in the water. The scales of the coelacanth are like hard armor plate, as were the scales of most prehistoric fish, to protect them from enemies.

The coelacanth isn't the only ancient species of fish discovered in this century. A few years ago a prehistoric looking fish was caught in Mariaville Lake, New York. It was four feet long, weighed 50 lbs. and had red wolf-like teeth. Thus far, this mystery fish has not been identified. Another new fish was discovered in 1964 by the research crew of the vessel JOHN ELLIOTT PILLSBURY off the coast of Florida. The one-inch black creature was named "Kasidoron edom" and is thought to be a member of the angler family. In Pyramid Lake, Nevada, divers recently rediscovered a sucker fish called "cui-ui." The cui-ui has lived for millions of years in the lake but can be found nowhere else in the world. This prehistoric fish had been the main diet for Nevada Indians for centuries.

The first fish appeared in this world about 350 million years ago. They were armor skinned creatures with large teeth but they couldn't swim and were forced to crawl the ocean bottom. An offshoot of these prehistoric fish is the sea robin and sculpin that still walk along the ocean bottom searching for food and they remain poor swimmers. The lumpfish, a close cousin to the sea robin and sculpin, has a hard sucking disc under its chin which is used to clamp itself to bottom rocks. The lumpfish hardly ever swims, but travels from rock to rock, using its nature-made suction cup to secure itself to the ocean floor. Some bottom fish swallow rocks and weight themselves to the bottom and scientists are a bit baffled about this action. Some of these fish seem to sense a brewing storm many days before it hits. The fish swallow stones to avoid being tossed around in rough seas and fishermen of the Atlantic and Gulf have reported catching fish with rocks in their bellies one week before a hurricane. In India, a fish called "misgurn," or European loach, is kept in aquariums at seismological stations throughout the country. These fish panic when an earthquake is about to strike and they dart about their tanks frantically hours before the scientists have any other warning that an earthquake is about to erupt.

Instead of swallowing rocks to weight itself down, the porcupine fish swallows water and air to buoy itself up when in danger. The porcupine fish has also perfected its armor into thorny sharp spines that cover its head and body and in some members of this family, the spines contain a potent neurotoxin that can cause swift death to other fish. This one to two-foot fish appears to be quite unassuming as it swims about the coral reefs, but if swallowed, even by a fish ten times its size, it will suck in water and blow itself up like a balloon, forcing the aggressor fish to either spit it out or choke to death. Cousins of the porcupine fish are the globe fish, boxfish and puffer fish and they all have similar defense mechanisms.

The boxfish is shaped like a tiny jewel box and has a bulb-like tail. It is a terrible swimmer and compared to other fish is looks very awkward in the depths but it also can swell up into a large ball four times its size. The puffer fish, called "dioden" in Australia, besides having the ability to puff itself up with water, squirts a toxic fluid from its mouth, blinding any aggressor fish. When swallowed by another fish it not only inflates itself and spits belly aching fluid, but gnaws its way out of the fish's stomach with its sharp, needle-like teeth. In the South Pacific the melon-shaped globe fish is called "tetrodon mbu" and it also inflates and deflates itself at will. In Japan, puffer fish is considered a delicacy, yet from 1927 to 1951 over 1,100 people died from eating puffers. The toxic flesh of the porcupine fish also recently caused two food poisoning deaths in Florida. Therefore, as tasty as they may be, it's suggested that inflatable fish should not be eaten.

One prehistoric fish that still swims the oceans of the world is the jellyfish. In fact, it was possibly the first swimming creature on earth. These soft bodied,

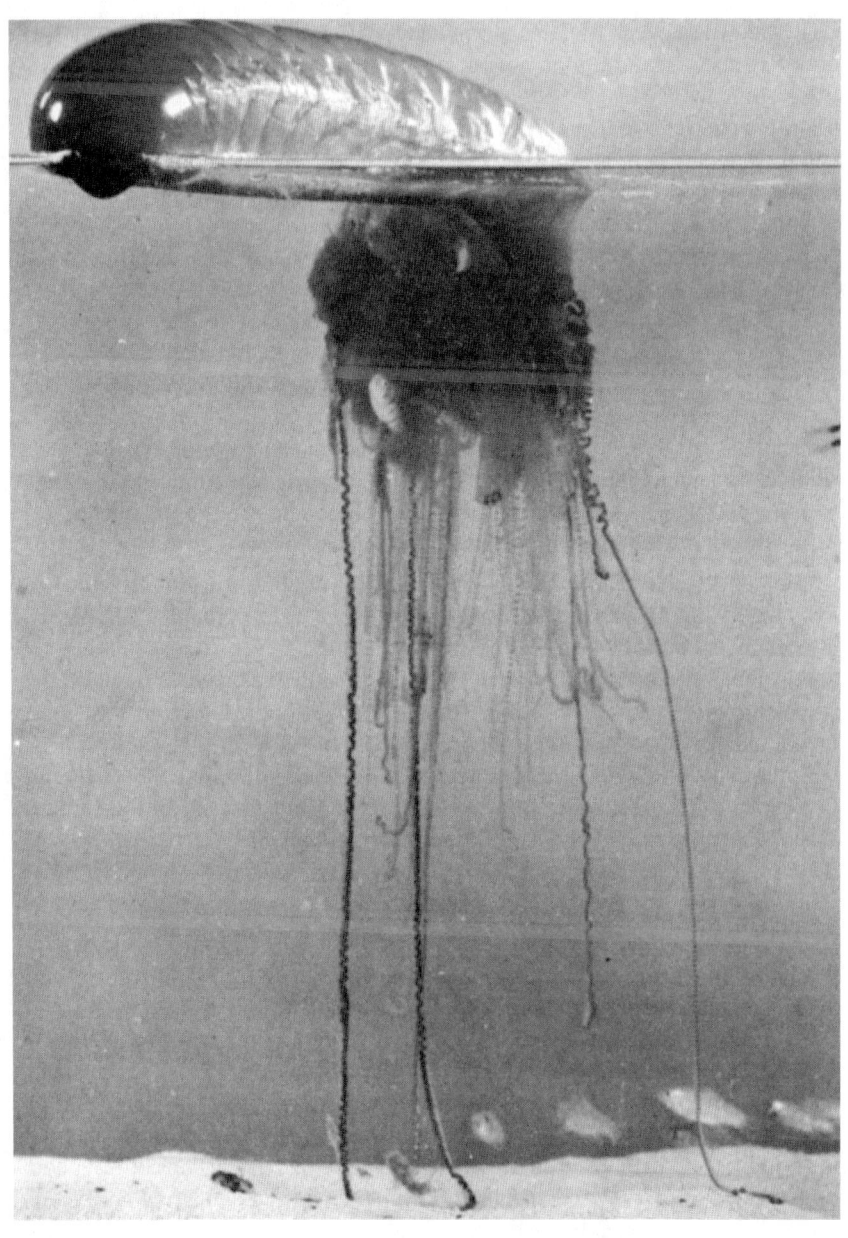

The deadly Portuguese Man-of-war, a dangerous colony of sea animals, all living under one jellowy roof.

often transparent creatures are made up of 98 percent water, yet they are one of the most dangerous animals in the sea. In Australia the jellyfish, which is also called a sea wasp, has caused more deaths than sharks. Within the last two years, nine Australians have been killed by these jellyfish and presently three Australian divers are allowing themselves to be stung by sea wasps in an experimental attempt to find an antidote for the deadly poison in their tentacles. These stinging jellyfish are sometimes no bigger than a penny but can grow to a size as big as a beach ball.

While I was skin-diving in the Red Sea one day in 1959, a school of giant jellyfish invaded the waters. All of them were about four feet in diameter. Swimming at a distance of some ten feet from one, I received an itchy, prickly feeling all over my body that forced me from the water. Although the jellyfish I encountered did not have long streaming tentacles, the tentacles of some jellyfish can extend some 25 feet from its inverted bowl-like body. In these many stinging tentacles are powerful toxins that can paralyze and kill humans. They sometimes use these tentacles to wrap around their victims, but most often jellyfish, like the sea wasp, puncture their prey with their stingers. A smaller member of the stinging jellyfish family is the sea nettle. It carries minute barbs loaded with poison, but they are not potent enough to cause serious injury to humans. The sting from a sea nettle will however, produce red welts that will remain on a human victim for days. Sea nettles, like most of the jellyfish family, usually swim on or near the surface and often invade beaches. Jellyfish in larva form attach themselves to the ocean bottom and before reaching maturity, their mouths are on top of their bodies rather than underneath, where they are located later in life. There also are fresh water jellyfish that grow no bigger than one inch and are found mostly in man-made bodies of water such as flooded ditches and quarries. The fresh water variety is not dangerous to man.

The most dangerous jellyfish in the sea is the Portuguese man-of-war, also known as "Physalia." It has long stinging tentacles that extend to 60 feet from its body and contains a poison that can terminate human life on contact. The Portuguese man-of-war is not just one fish, but a colony of little animals called polyps that perform various duties necessary to make this living sailing vessel function. The man-of-war looks like a miniature 15th century Portuguese galleon under full sail, thus the name. It also maneuvers like a sailing ship with its colorful bladder jutting some six inches above the surface waters to catch the wind, and its long tentacles, which can be lowered or retracted at will, operate as a rudder and sea anchor to prevent being beached.

The man-of-war continuously sails the tropical seas, blown by winds and currents, sometimes in convoys of over one thousand. Occasionally these man-of-war fleets have ventured out of warm waters and have driven swimmers ashore as far north as New England. Only one fish, the "nomeus-gronovi" has befriended the man-of-war and moves along the surface waters with it, feeding on any crumbs the jellyfish leaves behind. Although the nomeus is allowed to enter the poisonous domain of the man-of-war, it is not immune to its stingers. If it makes a wrong move the long tentacles will paralyze it permanently. Therefore the nomeus lives a most perilous day to day life. Even if a man-of-war is chopped into tiny pieces, each small particle has the ability to sting and possibly kill. Marine biologist Charles Lane, who first isolated man-of-war toxin and found it a beneficial antibiotic, also discovered that man-of-war venom can penetrate rubber gloves and even when frozen and dried, the tiny particles retain their stinging power.

As the man-of-war is often considered one of the most dangerous inhabitant of the sea, the piranha has won the distinction of being the most ferocious fresh water fish. These four to 14 inch razor-toothed creatures will attack any wounded fish or animal and quickly devour it, but recent evidence indicates that they may not be as mean as they're made out to be. In South America there are many gruesome tales of people being torn to pieces by piranha as they attempt to cross rivers. One Bolivian story tells about a native fisherman who pricked his finger on a thorn bush and walked down to the river to wash his wound. When he lifted his hand from the soothing water, only a stump remained. The piranha had eaten the flesh from his hand without him feeling a thing. In Brazil, because of piranha, cowboys have a difficult time deciding where to cross their cattle from one river bank to the other. Often they will cut

The great-barracuda waits for a meal to swim by, hovering over a giant brain coral off the Florida Keys. Cudas have been known to attack skin-divers and fishermen.
Photo by Paul Tzimoulis

the leg of their oldest steer and make it swim the river downstream where the piranha will reduce it to a skeleton within minutes. Meanwhile, the cowboys successfully cross the remainder of the herd upstream. There are also stories that many animals that drink from rivers and streams where piranha live, inevitably find themselves without tongues.

Dr. Hubert Markl, German ethnologist from the University of Frankfurt, recently announced that "piranha are timid fish that will not attack unless an object is abnormal looking and they will hesitate to attack anything bigger than themselves." Recently safaris to South America by scuba divers and marine scientists have shed some light on the true behavior of these supposedly man-eating fish. These explorers have all agreed that piranha will attack if there is blood in the water but otherwise, they are as tame as any other fish. Scuba divers have roamed the river bottoms with hundreds of piranha swimming around them and although the divers were unnerved by the many toothy grins, the piranha didn't so much as nibble. These explorers also discovered that piranha is a good tasting fish, "much like halibut," reported diver Dick Smith.

For a few years piranhas were imported into America for aquarium pets but the Department of Fish and Game soon put a stop to this, fearing that these so-called man-eaters would be deposited in local streams and begin breeding. Presently a chemical called "rotenone" is being used to kill off piranhas in Brazilian waters. This poison destroys piranha but does not affect other fish in the rivers.

A fish that is often called "the piranha of the sea" is the barracuda. Some believe this thin, toothy creature is more dangerous than the shark, but available evidence proves otherwise. In the last 100 years there have been 33 authenticated barracuda attacks and only four deaths can be directly attributed to this fish. The reason why barracuda attacks are not as fatal as shark attacks is because the barracuda will usually just bite once then leave the scene, whereas the shark will usually return to finish the job. However, with its jagged tiger-like teeth, the one bite from a barracuda can be substantial. One diver, Chispa Davis, was recently attacked while spearfishing of Andersen Island, Columbia. Davis had taken a shot at the three-foot cuda and missed. It then streaked at him "like a flash" and took a chunk of flesh out of his thigh. A few years ago in Biscayne Bay, a Miami hotel elevator operator swimming from Miami to Miami Beach had his arm bitten off by a barracuda.

Barracudas have extremely poor eyesight and are attracted to silvery or flashy objects. They are also curious creatures and will swim up close to investigate any unusual objects, such as a scuba diver. During the two years I spent exploring the Red Sea, two to three-foot barracudas would swim with me and I soon got used to their presence in the water, but one day, while probing the remains of a sunken freighter off Massawa, Eritrea, an eight-foot barracuda, called a "cuda-bear" joined diver Ron Hall and me. The giant cuda put a good scare into us as it circled and continuously moved its jaw as if chewing tobacco, displaying six inch long fangs. Its curiosity satisfied, it soon swam away. That same year, 1959, scuba diver Robert Straughan had a similar experience, only he had two eight-footers join him in the depths off Miami, Florida. Straughan's problem was that no one would believe that he encountered such large cudas, for at that time, the largest barracuda ever seen or caught was less than six feet long. It weighed 100 lbs., but was considered a monster freak. Most cudas are no bigger than three feet and don't weigh more than 40 lbs. Straughan's skeptics were satisfied two years later, when diver Bob Zimmerman caught two giant cudas off Miami and they both measured over eight feet. In 1994, a 12-footer was captured off the South coast of Africa.

At Saint Petersburg Beach, Florida in July of 1993, there were three separate attacks by barracudas on fishermen within four weeks. Fishing with a friend from a boat 14 miles off the coast, Bob Martin was mauled in the arm by a four-footer that jumped from the sea some ten feet into the boat deck. It clamped onto his arm with razor-sharp teeth and tore off a chunk of flesh which required 24 stitches. The very next day, another four-foot barracuda leaped into a houseboat, biting the hand and hip of a Tampa woman, which required 170 stitches to heal the wounds. On July 30, the fishing boat SLO-START was attacked by another four-footer, when it leaped into the boat trying to catch a snapper that was being reeled in. "He came out of the water like a rocket," said skipper Scharf Turner, "and launched right into the console, leaving the boat powerless, seven miles out to sea." The cuda tried to bite Tina DuPuy who had hooked the snapper, "but his snapping jaws missed me by a whisker," she later reported. Turner finally was able to kill the thrashing cuda with a club, but only after suffering a bite to the hand.

A fresh water cousin of the barracuda is the Northern pike. It will attack ducks and other birds that rest on the surface waters and in February of 1966, British newspapers reported that a pike attacked two dogs in a London reservoir and pulled them underwater. The pike, like the barracuda is an excellent tasting fish, but on occasion, barracuda taken from the tropical Atlantic and Pacific have caused ciguatera food poisoning when consumed. The reason for this is that barracuda sometimes eat toxic plants and fish and the toxins remain in its system.

There are other fish in addition to the piranha and barracuda that are notorious for their sharp teeth. The teeth of the blacktail fish for example, are exact miniature duplicates of human teeth and like the teeth of the gilt-head, they are so strong that they can crush fish hooks. The tough blue colored teeth of the gaudy wrasse will easily crack open seashells and the lumpfish and parrot fish have vice-like jaws that crush hard coral to dust. After chomping on coral all day, the parrot fish often visits the wrasse or baby butterfly fish to have its teeth cleaned. The wrasse and butterfly actually climb inside the parrot fish mouth and peck away at any remaining morsels of food. The lip fish also cleans teeth and sets up cleaning stations on the sea bottom where the larger fish visit periodically. There are other fish such as the Northern perch, that clean the skin of other fish and eat any and all parasites that are clinging to the larger fish. When a giant sunfish approaches a school of Northern perch, it rolls over and closes its eyes as the perch soothe the giant into slumber by pecking parasite worms from its body.

The hungry sea-slug allows the "fierasfer fish" inside its mouth, but not for the purpose of cleaning teeth. The fierasfer enters the slug's mouth to bait other fish. When other fish follow the fierasfer they are eaten by the sea-slug. Meanwhile, the fierasfer hides in the sea-slug's stomach and eats the leftovers. Then if pops out of the slug's mouth to lure in more suckers. There are other small fish like the fierasfer that act as barkers to beckon victims into the mouths of larger fish and as a reward, they are fed and protected by the larger fish. Even some school fish have a protector, for example the herring schools often rely on the sea-cat to frighten off larger fish. This strange looking, somewhat shark-like fish grows to three or four times larger than the herring but is allowed to swim freely with them. The sea-cat has wing-like fins and its eyes shine in the dark. It also has a fleshy knob that looks like a crown located between its eyes and fishermen have aptly dubbed the sea-cat "King Herring."

Fish that don't have a protector find a variety of ways to hide themselves from predators. The flounder flicks sand onto its back with its tail until all but its eyes are covered with a blanket of sand. The goby constructs a hiding place out of sand by secreting a cement-like substance through its skin that hardens the sand and produces a fish-made cave. The little transparent fish called the "sand diver" spends most of its life buried in the sand to avoid being eaten and the Siamese fish burrows into the mud and lives there for three to four months of each year. The West Coast geoduck fish lives some three feet under the mud where bigger fish can't get at it.

Some Arctic fish avoid being eaten by entrapping themselves in blocks of ice. The six inch Alaskan blackfish can remain frozen for weeks and when the ice thaws it swims away. The skin tissue of the blackfish has a lower freezing point than water and therefore it survives the ice enclosure. Marine scientist David Jordon, while studying fish life in Alaska, reported that a frozen blackfish was fed to a Husky dog and two minutes later he saw the surprised dog cough up a live and squirming fish. It had thawed out in the dog's warm stomach. There are other fish as well that can survive 1.7 degree below zero water temperatures and one fish, the "teleost," can live in hot tropical waters as well as cold, 1.8 degree water temperatures, making it one of the most versatile fish in the world. The cichlid fish on the other hand lives in the hot springs of Lake Magadi, Kenya, Africa, with temperatures that vary from 80 to 115 degrees but cannot survive extremely cold water. The Alaskan smelt, also known as "candlefish," survives extremely cold water and cannot live in warm water. The flesh of the candlefish is filled with oil, and Alaskan Indians not only eat them with relish, but often dry them, shove a wick through the flesh and use them as candles.

The most common function for protection in the sea is for fish to move from one place to another in formation. Many large fish avoid a school of smaller fish because the school often appears to them like one great monster. When the predator attacks, the schooling fish move closer together, and moving as a well drilled unit they dart one way and then the other in an effort to escape. The fate of any straggler in the school is inevitable. Eyesight is extremely important to school fish and experiments have shown that partially blind fish drift away from the school because they are unable to keep up with the others. Fish rely on their eyesight to properly position themselves in the rank and file of a school and at night, schools tend to break down because one fish can't keep its eye on the movement of another.

Most fish are nearsighted but they have good wide angle vision, allowing them to see in many directions at one time. However, since most fish search for food at dawn and hide during daylight hours, nearsightedness is probably not a great handicap. Flying fish can see out of water as well as in and their corneas are shaped like three-sided pyramids, allowing them to see forward, backward and down at the same time. The archer fish that sticks its head above surface waters to spit at bugs, can also see fairly well out of water, but most fish can't see more than a blur when they are taken from water. In the water, members of the seahorse and pipefish family can move their eyes independently of one another and can look forward and backward at the same time. One specie of South American fish has eyes that are divided into upper and lower sections and while cruising the surface waters it can see above and below water at the same time.

The flounder begins life swimming in an upright position and looks much like any other fish, but as it matures, its mouth and one eye move to the top of its head. This gives the face of the flounder a twisted look but allows it to feed on the bottom while at the same time keeping a lookout above. Jellyfish can only tell light from dark, and cave fish, such as the characin, have eyes when they're young but as they mature their eyes loose vision and they become totally blind. Some fish like the butterfly and mock-eye fish have false eyes on their tails. These are merely black markings that look like eyes, but when an enemy attacks it mistakes the tail for the head and when the mock-eye fish darts forward it leaves the attacker somewhat bewildered.

University of Maryland scientists have recently discovered that parrot fish use their eyes to follow the sun as a means of undersea navigation. Parrot fish travel across vast sandy bottoms in search of coral to feed on and in these sunken deserts there is no way for the fish to find their direction back and forth without using the sun. The scientists moved some parrot fish to unfamiliar waters, attached one end of a nylon line to their fins and the other end to a surface balloon which allowed them to observe the fish movements from the surface. On sunny days the parrot fish swam southeasterly using the sun as a compass, but on cloudy days the fish became confused and would discontinue their journey until the sun reappeared.

Redfish come into shallow water to feed in the early morning but as the sun comes out they retreat into the depths. It's thought that one reason for this behavior is that the sun, as it becomes brighter, hurts their eyes. In Obscure Imperial Reservoir, Texas, where redfish have been successfully transplanted from saltwater to fresh, the habit of the shy redfish is the same. A most unusual transplant of redfish took place in 1928, when four coastal English towns were caught in a tremendous rainstorm. Along with the raindrops came a downpour of redfish. Apparently a school of redfish had been caught in an ocean waterspout, lifted up into the sky, were swallowed by a cloud and were dropped with the rain.

Since fish do not have eyelids, some ichthyologists have concluded that fish do not sleep, but other marine scientists have refuted this theory with the comment, "Fish do not have ears either, yet they can hear." A few species however, do have ears inside their head and these include the eel, goldfish, catfish, and minnow. One fish that does sleep is the parrot fish and to protect itself during slumber it secretes a slimy mucus through its skin which apparently is distasteful to other fish. Some bottom fish wedge themselves into coral caves to catch a few winks and some school fish drift together with the currents as they slumber. Certain species like the mackerel and tuna must keep swimming or they will sink and it is assumed that these fish do not sleep. Therefore, we can only conclude that some fish do sleep while others may not require sleep, or maybe they just take a few cat naps now and then.

One of the first men to realize that fish do hear was a 17th century Austrian monk who would ring a bell at a river bank each day to beckon his pet trout to dinner. Fish that do not have ears can sense noise through their skin, much like we can feel the rumble of a distant explosion in our feet but might not actually hear it. The lateral line running down both sides of most fish is a sixth sense organ that allows them to hear various low vibrations as well as loud noises. This auxiliary ear often warns them of approaching danger before they can see it and also allows them to communicate with each other. The sea horse for example, makes a clucking noise with its mouth that sounds somewhat like our Morse Code and is heard and understood by its own kind. Toadfish communicate with each other with a series of whistles and some species grind their teeth, setting up vibrations that can be understood by others through the lateral lines in their skin. Thusfar it is believed that these signals between fish are either mating calls or warnings of approaching danger, but their communications may be more complex than we presently understand.

Many fish also have the ability to detect food and enemies through a sense of smell and many recent experiments have concluded that most fish have a better sense of smell than we do. For example, when minnows were blindfolded they quickly swam away from the scent of their natural enemy the pike, even though the pike was dropped into the water many yards away from them. Although fish don't have noses, they do have nostrils that are located near their eyes. Most fish also have taste buds that are located in their tongues but they cannot distinguish anything beyond bitter or salty foods. This limited taste ability is probably responsible for the reputation that fish have of eating strange objects. In the last few years, many trout have been caught that had cigarette filters in their stomachs and the tops of flip-top cans lodged in their digestive tracts. In 1968, Steven Gamash of Athol, Massachusetts, lost his eye glasses while swimming and later that same day, while fishing, caught a trout with his glasses in its mouth. Many rings and other small gadgets have been found in the stomachs of fish and a most unusual coincidence occurred in Paris, France in 1903. Mrs. Eduigue Rerrit dropped her ring down a kitchen drain and five days later when she bought a fish for supper at the local market and cut it open, she found her ring in its stomach.

The carp is noted for its habit of eating just about anything and recently the Soviet Union imported thousands of them from China to solve a pressing problem. The water ways of Russia were clogged with weeds, hindering water traffic. The carp were imported to eat the weeds and thusfar they have done wonders in helping to solve the problem. After the Soviet success, Britain imported 15,000 carp from Hong Kong to clear away weeds from the clogged inlets leading to power plants. The weeds were stopping the flow of water into the plants and the carp soon came to the rescue and are responsible for keeping the lights burning in England.

Among the more greedy fish is the Betta or Siamese fighting fish. It can eat twice its own weight in a day and besides being a glutton, it has a nasty disposition. When two Bettas of the same sex are placed in a tank together, they will fight to the death. Battles between Bettas have been known to last six hours until one kills the other. A recent fad at college fraternities was weekly bouts between these fish. At Nevada University they even charged admission and gave the fish such names as "The Rock" and "Reggie The Ripper." In one championship fight, the audience demanded their money back when the two fish wouldn't fight and it was soon discovered that the champs were of opposite sexes.

Whether a fish is a fighter or a coward, a school fish or one that remains in a fixed neighborhood, it lives in a cruel world of eat or be eaten. Fish are continuously frightened and well they should be, for only one out of some 10 million escapes a violent death. In fact, fish worry so much that many of them, like humans, have ulcers. An examination of 42 marlin caught during the 1970

A scientist from the New England Aquarium inspects a 450 pound giant squid that washed ashore at Newburyport, Massachusetts in 1980. Its body was 12-feet long with 16 foot tentacles.

Scuba diver taunts an octopus out of its cave. These little creatures may be the most intelligent denizens of the deep.
Photo by Ron Church.

Hawaiian Billfish Tournament revealed that six of the fish were suffering from severe ulcers, similar to those found in humans.

Based on the above, we can conclude that fish have many of the traits, abilities and habits that we humans do. They worry, have memories, are victims of habit, choose their leaders, love sex, communicate with each other, can taste, smell, hear and see, and just as some of us know how to swim, some of them can walk on land and a few have perfected flying and jet propulsion. One thing of course is that fish do not have the ability to think as we do, but some scientists are not completely convinced of this. Recent thought provoking studies of the brain of the octopus and grouper have revealed that these fellows are pretty smart. Possibly the only conclusion we can come to is that fish don't have religion. Yet, there are certain religious symbols in the sea that should not be overlooked.

There is a fish found in abundance off the coast of Norway that has a human, angelic face and a layer of flesh over its head that looks exactly like a hood. Because of its holy appearance it is called the sea monk. There is also a salt water fish called a sail cat that has a body formed like a crucifix and has a natural sword-like bone plunged into the side of its body. The back of the sail cat resembles a Roman shield and when caught, the fish rattles like the dice that were thrown at the foot of Christ's cross. Another strange little fish was recently netted off the coast of Nicaragua and is thought to be a distant relative of the manta ray. Only ten inches tall, it has the face of a human with slanty eyes and a scowl. It had two horns protruding from its head and a long narrow tail with a point at its tip and to complete its devilish appearance, it had fins shaped like hands and feet. One wonders if mother nature created these symbols of good and evil in the sea for the fish, or for us?

II
MULTI-ARMED MARVELS

The ugliest creature in the sea is the octopus. It is also one of the most unpredictable. There are hundreds of reports of octopuses attacking bathers, divers and fishermen, especially off the coasts of Italy, Ireland, France and Northwest America, areas where these multi-armed creatures may be found in abundance. There are also stories of encounters with friendly, even shy octopus. We therefore must assume that some of these creatures have friendly dispositions, whereas others are openly aggressive, or that octopuses, like us humans, have varying moods.

In the 17th century, most people thought the octopus was an imaginary creature, yet during this same period, it was generally believed that mermaids existed. Today, we realize that the beauty is fiction and the beast is fact, but there still remain many misconceptions about the octopus and its cousins, the squid, cuttlefish and nautilus.

These creatures have been around for a long time. Fossils of members of the octopus family have been found in Cambrian rocks, some of them dating back 400 million years and today are among the oldest fossils ever discovered. There were also giant ancestors of the octopus living in the primeval seas of the world, wearing 15-foot cone-shaped shells. In those days there were some 3,000 species of "nautiloids" or octopus. Today, there are approximately 150 species of octopus in the underwater world, varying in size from two inches to 32 feet or more. The average size squid is from 12 to 20 inches long, yet giant squid grow to a length of 70 feet and some have been captured close to this size. In October, 1875, the schooner HOWARD came upon five giant squid dead on the surface waters at the Grand Banks, off New England. The body of the largest one, not including its tentacles, was 15 feet long. Another ship at The Banks captured a live squid that same week. Its body was 36 feet long and it had 35-foot long tentacles. The giant squid is the largest animal in the world without a back bone.

The small cuttlefish is the only member of this multi-armed family that does have a back bone, and a very popular bone it is. Cuttlebone is used by school children as pencil erasers and is often seen in bird cages for canaries and parakeets to sharpen their beaks on. In powdered form, it is used in toothpastes, and in medicines as an ingredient in antacids and skin disease lotions. It is used as a polishing powder by jewelers and recently in France, it was discovered that cuttlebone was used by thieves to make molds for counterfeit franc pieces.

Another little member of the family, the female nautilus, sometimes called an argonaut, wears a paper-thin shell. Unlike the octopus that can walk on the bottom or swim at will, the paper nautilus never touches the ocean bottom, but drifts with the currents near the surface. They travel in schools of 100 or more and are rarely seen, for they feed in deeper water during the day and come to the surface at night. Sailors once considered their presence on the surface waters as an omen of good luck, and once in a while a nautilus will even secrete valuable pearls. The shell of the female nautilus is used as a hydrostatic organ, allowing it to regulate its desired depth. How this pressurized system of air chambers works, nobody actually knows. The male paper nautilus doesn't have a shell and he grows to only one-tenth the size of the female. A cousin of the paper nautilus, called the chambered nautilus, lives in the western Pacific at depths up to 2,000 feet and comes to the surface infrequently. The paper nautilus has eight arms or tentacles like the octopus, but the male chambered nautilus has about 60 arms and the female has up to 94 arms, and the arms of the chambered variety do not have suckers.

Each arm of the octopus has 240 disc-shaped suckers, each acting as an individual suction cup. It is no wonder that, with the total of 1,920 of these pressurized discs, the common octopus is considered one of the strongest creatures in the sea. When an octopus has a firm grip on an object, even if its arm is torn off, the suckers will remain. Many large sperm whales that have been captured were covered with platter-size welts received from battles with their arch enemy the giant squid. Even the bellies of whales have displayed circular scars from squid that had been swallowed alive. In 1950, a 35-foot squid was taken from the stomach of a 47-foot sperm whale off the Azores. Unlike the octopus and paper nautilus, the squid and cuttlefish have ten arms. This extra set of tentacles are long and more slender and can be withdrawn into pockets located behind the creature's head. There is also a species of octopus, discovered in the Arctic Ocean in 1958, that has 40 arms.

None of the above multi-armed creatures are scientifically considered fish. They all belong to the family of marine cephalopod mollusks, and although "cephalopod" means "head footed," every member of the family is a blue-blood. The blue color results from a copper compound in the blood. Most members of this family, except for the chambered nautilus, have been blessed with two kidneys, two gills and three hearts. If an octopus or squid should lose an arm in combat, another grows in its place. The octopus can regrow a lost arm within six weeks. These creatures can also regenerate a damaged eye and some scientists believe that they can regenerate a completely lost eye. As the creature itself grows older and bigger it, like the lobster, sheds its skin for a new layer.

Octopuses live in all oceans of the world and can be found at varying depths, from the shallows to over 14,000 feet. An octopus was fished up from 2,425 fathoms in the Arctic in 1932. It was transparent, had the consistency of a jellyfish, and was totally blind.

Most octopuses have keen eyesight and their eyes closely resemble the human eye in every detail. Yet, octopuses seem to like darkness. They usually live in caves and crevices and they do most of their hunting for food at night. Diver Jacques Cousteau tells us that while retrieving ancient amphorae (wine jugs) from a Greek merchant ship that sank off Marseilles centuries ago, almost every jug they brought to the surface had an octopus living in it. "The wreck and the amphorae had been " 'octopied' for centuries," said Cousteau. Japanese salvagers in 1856 actually used octopuses to recover pottery from a sunken ship. The wreck with the valuables aboard was too deep for divers, so they tied leashes to octopuses and dropped them over the side of their salvage ship. The octopuses were lowered to the deck of the sunken ship and instinctively crawled inside the pieces of pottery. With suction cups firmly attached to the inside of each valuable item, the creatures were hauled to the surface. The entire cargo was thus salvaged by this octopus-on-the-line method.

There are many stories, some exaggerated, of divers encountering octopuses in the dark recesses of sunken ships and in other man-made debris that clutters the ocean bottoms. British diver Henry Bruce once came upon a pair of overalls at a depth of 40 feet off Gibraltar. "I was shocked," said Bruce, "that as I bent down to pick up the overalls, they picked up and ran off before my eyes." Living inside the pair of overalls, Bruce discovered, was an octopus. Apparently, the octopus was quite upset with the intrusion of its privacy, for it attacked Bruce and he was forced to kill it with his knife.

Fishermen have also netted octopuses living inside dark objects such as barrels, shells and cans. In the summer of 1899, an Atlantic fisherman netted a human skull with an octopus living inside it. Marine scientist L. R. Brightwell was aboard an English Channel trawler in the 1950's when an octopus was netted. At the time, Brightwell was more interested in some of the other marine animals that were being captured, and he momentarily forgot about the octopus. When he finally searched the deck for the little fellow, it was nowhere in sight. Brightwell and members of the crew searched the ship for two hours before the octopus was found. Retracing its steps, they discovered that it had walked across the deck, climbed down the companionway and crawled into the galley. They found it cowering in the tea kettle on the stove.

It is obvious from Mr. Brightwell's experience that octopuses can travel out of water as well as in it. Natives of the Pacific Islands have seen the creatures come out of the water to attack rats and even climb trees to obtain fruit. Some even claim that for short distances, an octopus can run faster than a man. In Southern California, octopuses come out of the water at night to crawl over the mud flats looking for food. At a beach in Scarborough, England, in the summer if 1925, local newspapers reported that an octopus chased a dog up four flights of seaside stone steps. The octopus caught the dog and almost succeeded in dragging it into the sea. A fisherman tried to rescue the dog and he too was almost pulled under. Finally, other fishermen rushed to the scene and killed the octopus, which was reported to weigh some 20 to 30 pounds.

The "Weekly Oregonian" in September, 1877, reported that a woman was dragged off an Oregon beach and pulled underwater by a giant octopus. Indian divers attempted to rescue the woman by attacking the creature underwater with knives. The octopus retreated and the Indians managed to drag the drowned woman ashore.

At an aquarium in Brighton, England some years ago, the keeper discovered that night after night, fish were disappearing from their tanks. There was no apparent reason for the vanishing fish, so the keeper remained in the aquarium one night and he watched in amazement as an octopus climbed out of its tank, slid across the floor and invaded the other tanks for a midnight snack. Keeper Julius Kallman of the Naples Zoological Station, once placed a large lobster in a tank with an octopus, but the two fought continuously and Kallman had to separate them. He placed the lobster in a separate tank, where the octopus couldn't see it. Yet, one night, the octopus climbed out of its own tank, crept across the floor and into the lobster's tank. In the morning, Kallman found the octopus chewing happily on large chunks of lobster meat. Another story of a night walking cephalopod is told by the keeper of a Bermuda aquarium. This little creature managed to squeeze between the glass tank and the lid of the tank, a space no more than two inches thick. It then proceeded to walk across the floor, down the steps and out the front door of the building. It managed to crawl 100 feet in the direction of the beach before it dropped dead. The keeper found it in the morning, partially eaten by ants.

All octopuses are jelly-like in substance, and even the bulkiest of the family can squeeze through paper-thin cracks and crevices. They have the ability to flatten their bodies and literally ooze their way through. Marine scientists love to tell the story about one of their colleagues who captured a 13-inch octopus in a tidal pool, put it in a basket, tied down the lid of the basket and headed for the laboratory. While sitting in the subway with the basket on the seat beside him, the scientist heard an ear-piercing scream from the other end of the car. There sitting on a hysterical lady's lap was his octopus.

Multi-armed marvels can also perform other feats of magic such as changing the color and texture of their skin to blend in with surroundings. This camouflage is so effective that divers have peered into octopus caves without seeing the creatures lurking within. Another disappearing act is performed by octopuses when they discharge an inky fluid causing an undersea smoke-screen which allows them to retreat unnoticed. Baby octopuses discharge their first squirt of ink before birth. It usually happens when they are angrily trying to fight the unyielding egg case. The ink, which has a unique, musty odor, is said to momentarily cause fish to lose their sense of smell. It is also, in strong doses, fatal to fish and to the octopus as well. It is interesting to note that deep-sea squid, living in the black bowels of the ocean, also have this remarkable defense mechanism, but instead of black ink, they eject a luminous fluid which dazzles attackers.

Ink from the octopus, cuttlefish and squid is sold commercially by fishermen to industrial and creative artists. It is called "sepia ink" and varies in colors from dark-brown (squid) to blue (cuttlefish) to black (octopus). Ink from cephalopods, fossilized for over 100 million years, can still be diluted and used by artists today.

The mouth of the squid and the octopus is protected by a horny beak, resembling somewhat a parrot beak and is used to drill holes through sea shells. This beak is probably the most important tool to the octopus, for its favorite foods — abalone, clams, crabs, oysters and lobsters — all live in shells. Once the octopus has pecked through a shell it can easily suck out the flesh and fluid. Except when fighting or feeding, the beak is retracted into the creature's mouth. In addition, the octopus can secrete a venom through its beak, which can paralyze and sometimes kill its victims. This toxic fluid also softens the flesh tissues allowing the octopus to sip the flesh into its small mouth.

Octopus venom can also be fatal to man. Fishermen in India fear a small octopus called "poisonous kanavai," because it is aggressive and often bites causing great pain and, on occasion, death to its victims. Recently, in Hawaii, there have been three near fatalities from octopus bites. In all three cases, the octopus was no more than a few inches long. One Hawaiian fisherman who found a small octopus in the shallows and picked it up, said that the bite was like a bee sting, and there was excessive bleeding from the pin-like wound. This fisherman suffered a dizzy spell for days and his hand was swollen and sore for over a week. There have been two recent deaths in Australia caused by octopus bites, and in both cases, the octopus was no bigger than a pack of cigarettes. At Melbourne, Australia, a man was paralyzed for eight hours after handling a small octopus caught off Rickett's Point. A doctor at the Melbourne Hospital diagnosed the man to be suffering from acute poisoning. When he regained consciousness he said that he had felt no sting from the octopus, but had noticed a speck of blood on the back of his hand and he collapsed a short time later.

If all these weapons and defense mechanisms weren't enough, nature also provided the octopus with jet propulsion. Squids, cuttlefish and octopus can streak through the water with the greatest of ease and can outswim most of their undersea enemies. They do so by taking in ocean water and quickly forcing it out through a natural body funnel called a "siphon." Octopuses also use this siphon on land to shoot water at their victims, such as mice and rats, and they squirt water to wet down areas they intend to crawl through, which makes land travel easier for them. Many South Sea islanders have been hit with these jet streams while chasing octopuses along the beach. They report that an octopus can shoot a spout of water some ten feet into the air. Squids, considered one of the fastest marine animals, also use the siphons to rocket out of the water and glide over the waves. A ship cruising some 300 miles off the coast of Brazil once reported that over 100 squid shot out of the water and landed on the deck, 13 feet above the surface. Dr. Gilbert Voss, professor of marine science at the University of Miami, says that squids can rocket some 40 feet out of the water.

The squids of the Humboldt Current, off Peru and Chile, are feared by fisherman, not only because of their size (12 to 60 feet and weighing up to 1000 pounds), but also because they can leap out of the water to capture victims in their long, embracing tentacles. These squid can attack and strip a swordfish or giant tuna to the bone within a few minutes and they have been known to attack and even sink ships. The tanker BRUNSWICK, with a regular run between Hawaii and Samoa had a rare experience, between 1930 and 1933, of being attacked three times by giant squids. Norwegian executive Arne Groenningsaeter reports that each of the three squids was over 60 feet long and that they traveled at speeds of over 20 miles an hour. They always attacked from the bow and once, reaching approximately the middle of the ship, tried to wrap their tentacles around her. They finally gave up their attacks because the ship was too large for them to conquer.

In the Atlantic Ocean, off the Eastern end of Belle Isle in Conception Bay, Newfoundland, history records a squid attacking and almost capsizing a 20-foot boat on October 26, 1873. A creature with huge green eyes and a parrot-like beak, seized the small boat which contained two herring fishermen and a 12 year old boy named Tom Piccot. One fisherman struck the giant squid with a boat hook, and the creature started climbing aboard in an attempt to drag the boat under. Young Piccot picked up an axe and smashed at its tentacles. He managed to cut two of them off and the creature retreated into the depths in an inky cloud. Tom Piccot was the hero of the day and he recovered two 19-foot tentacles to prove to his pals that he and the fishermen weren't telling a tall tale.

A year later, May 10, 1874, a giant squid succeeded in sinking a ship. The skipper of the schooner PEARL reported the disaster in the July 5th issue of "News of the World" as follows:

"I was lately the skipper of the schooner PEARL, a 150 ton, tight little craft, with a crew of six men. We were bound from Mauritius to Rangoon, tin ballast to return with padding and had put into Galle for water. Three days out we fell becalmed into the bay, latitude 8 degrees 50 min. north, and longitude 84 degrees 5 min. east. At about 5:00pm we sighted a two-masted steamer on our port quarter, about five or six miles off. Very soon after, as we lay motionless, a great mass rose slowly out of the sea about a half mile off on our starboard side, and remained spread out and stationary. It looked like the back of a huge whale but sloped less, and was of a brownish color. Even at that distance it seemed much longer than our craft and it seemed to be basking in the sun.

"I went into the cabin for my rifle, and, as I was preparing to fire, Bill Darling, a Newfoundlander, came on deck, and looking at the monster, exclaimed, 'Have a care, that there's a squid, and will capsize us if we hurt him.' Smiling at the idea, I let fly...hit him and with that he shook. There was a great ripple all around him and he began to move.

" 'Out with your axes and knives,' shouted Bill, 'and cut any part of him that comes aboard; look alive and Lord help us!' "

"Not aware of the danger, and never having seen or heard of such a monster, I gave no orders, and it was no use touching the helm or ropes to get out of the way."

"By this time three of the crew, Bill included, had found axes, and all were looking over the ship's side at the advancing monster. We could see now a large oblong mass moving by jerks, just under the surface of the water, and an enormous train following; the oblong body was at least half the size of our vessel in length, and just as thick; the wake of the train might have been 100 feet long. In the time I have taken to write, the brute struck us, and the ship quivered under its thud; in another moment the monster was aboard, squeezed in between the masts. The brute, holding on by its arms, slipped its vast body overboard, and pulled the vessel down with it on her beam ends. Monstrous arms like trees seized the vessel and she reeled over. We were thrown into the water at once, and just as I went over, I caught sight of one of the crew, either Bill or Tom Fielding, squashed up between the masts in one of those awful arms. For a few seconds our ship lay on her beam ends, then filled and went down. Another of the crew must have been sucked down, for only five of us were picked up."

This statement was signed by James Floyd, late master of the schooner. One of the many passengers on the nearby steamer STRATHOWEN that saw the PEARL go under, gives the following report:

"Steering over a calm and tranquil sea. About an hour before sunset on May 10, we saw, on our starboard beam, and about two miles off, a small schooner, lying becalmed. As I examined her with my binoculars, and then noticed between us, but nearer to her, a long, low swelling, lying on the sea, which, from its color and shape, I took to be a bank of seaweed. The mass was then set in motion. It struck the schooner, which visibly reeled and then righted. Immediately afterwards the masts swayed sideways and with my glass I could clearly discern the enormous mass and hull of the schooner coalescing. The other gazers witnessed the same appearance. The schooner's masts swayed toward us, lower, lower, till the vessel was on her beam end. She lay there a few seconds and then disappeared. A cry of horror arose from the lookers on;

and, if by instinct, our ship's head was at once turned towards the scene and the sole survivors of the pretty little schooner. As soon as the poor fellows were able, they told us the story, stating that their vessel was submerged by a giant squid, the animal which, in smaller form, attracts so much attention in the Brighton (England) Aquarium as the octopus."

A year later, there was another giant squid attack off Connemara, Ireland. Three men in an open boat came upon an object in the water which looked like a "floating mass of seaweed." The object then embraced the boat in its arms. The crew, with only one knife among them, managed to chop off its limbs and finally its head. "The rest of the body sank at once," they reported. The battle with the squid lasted for over two hours and upon returning to shore, they showed the squid limbs to Sergeant Thomas O'Connor of the Royal Irish Constabulary. He, in turn, presented the captured arms and head to the Dublin Museum, where they remain preserved today. One of the tentacles on display measures 8 feet and a second arm measures 30 feet.

On November 30, 1853, the steamship ALECTON was cruising off the Canary Islands when a 50-foot squid surfaced in her path. A battle ensued, and crewmen harpooned the creature. It tried to capture them with its "ten" tentacles, but within an hour the crew managed to lasso the squid's tail. The tail was brought aboard, but the rope cut the creature in half, the head and tentacles sinking back into the depths. After weighing the tail, the crew estimated that the squid weighed approximately 4000 pounds, and was a least 60 feet long.

Many giant squid and octopus have been captured whole, such as the octopus that was cast ashore in Denmark after a storm in 1854. Its body measured 21 feet across. Its total length was 50 feet and its longest tentacle was 18 feet long. In that same year, one was found dead on a beach at Jutland, England, with twenty foot arms and a beak measuring 9 inches. The largest squid ever captured was one found stranded in the shallows off Newfoundland in November 1875. It was dragged ashore by fishermen, tied to a tree and when it died a few hours later, it was measured. Its arms were 35 feet long, and its overall length was 55 feet. Although local dogs ate most of the creature before scientists arrived on the scene, a replica of this monster is now on exhibit at the Smithsonian Institute in Washington, D.C.

Four fishermen entangled a giant squid in their nets off Logy Bay, Newfoundland, in 1873. The frightened fishermen stabbed at it and managed to bring the creature ashore. A local naturalist, Reverend Moses Harvey, bought the remains of the squid from the fisherman for $10.00. He and others dragged it to his home where he attempted to preserve it in an outhouse bath. Harvey astounded the scientific world when he reported that the beast was 32 feet long. Prior to this, scientists and naturalists didn't believe the stories about giant squid.

Giant squid are often found in the bellies of captured whales. A whale harpooned off Madeira in 1952 contained a live squid 34 feet long, weighing over 350 pounds. Squid is the favorite food of sperm whales, and it was only recently discovered that valuable ambergris is produced by the hard parrot-like beak of the squid, which the whale cannot digest. Scientists now believe that squid beaks become lodged in the whale's digestive tract causing an irritation which produces ambergris. Ambergris is used as a base for expensive perfumes.

On July 8, 1875, the captain and crew of the ship PAULINE had the rare experience of witnessing a battle between a whale and a giant squid. The captain, George Drevar and five crewmen describe the encounter as follows:

"We, the undersigned, observed three large sperm whales, and one was gripped round the body with two turns of what appeared to be a huge serpent. The head and tail appeared to have a length beyond the coils of about 30 feet, and its girth eight or nine feet. The serpent whirled its victim round and round for about 15 minutes, and then suddenly dragged the whale to the bottom, head first..."

It has been concluded that the "serpent" Captain Drevar described was actually a giant squid, since the sperm whale and the squid have been arch enemies, probably since primeval days. Although we know that whales eat squids, scientists are still not sure which giant beast is the predator. It could be assumed that since squids attack boats, which from beneath the surface appear to look like whales, giant squids are possibly the ferocious aggressors.

Squids, of course, have other enemies as well, such as the shark, porpoise, eels and penguins. A penguin captured off Antarctica was cut open to reveal 96 squid beaks in its stomach. There have been many fights between sharks and octopuses as well, some staged and some natural encounters. Being of equal size, the octopus usually wins the battle by squeezing the shark's gills closed with its tentacles. The vitality of squids and octopuses and their immunity to pain is amazing. An octopus can lose most of its limbs and still fight on. Even out of water, they have been known to walk through camp fires without seemingly feeling any worse for wear. An octopus will readily battle with another octopus, and they are cannibalistic even to the point of eating themselves. At the Zoological Station at Naples, a keeper witnessed an octopus eating five of its own arms, and recently at the West Berlin Aquarium, an octopus with six-foot tentacles ate itself to death, at the rate of half an inch per day. Scientists are puzzled at this unusual, yet not uncommon behavior. Usually octopuses adapt to captivity quickly and for the most part seem to enjoy living in aquarium tanks. Also, at no time was a self-devouring octopus in need or want of food and in fact, octopuses can live for weeks without food. Naturalists believe that an octopus destroys itself when under stress, but as yet, they haven't reasoned what it is that troubles an octopus so much that it will consume itself.

Humans in some parts of the world eat octopuses and squids as part of their diets, daily. The Japanese, Chinese and Italians could be considered the octopus' greatest enemies for they devour these creatures by the hundreds of thousands every year. Octopus meat is actually quite good, tasting somewhat like lobster, but a bit chewier. The dish calamari (fried octopus) is becoming quite popular in America.

In Naples, Italy, the heads of octopuses are displayed in the market as a high-priced food and in other parts of Italy hot octopus is sold whole on a stick from

This 18th century Norwgian woodcut depicts a "kraken' sinking a ship in 1752. A bishop aboard the ship reported that the monster "darkened the water around it with an inky excretion," which means that the "kraken" was a giant squid.

street vendors. It's not uncommon to see Italian women wearing necklaces made of octopus eyes. In Japan, octopus and squid are served in many ways. The tentacles are often served as an appetizer before dinner, like a shrimp cocktail. Japanese fishermen catch more squid and octopus than the fishermen of any other country. In squid alone, Japan consumes approximately 500,000 tons a year. Squids and octopuses are also sold for dog and cat food, and for fertilizer.

Fishermen usually capture these creatures in nets, but in Tahiti and the Gilbert Islands, natives have concocted unique methods of catching octopuses. Along the shores of Tahiti, skin-diver Wilman Menard lured them out of their shallow water caves by sitting on the shore playing his flute. The music apparently hypnotizes the octopuses and as they approach shore, this undersea pied piper drops his flute, picks up his spear and jabs them between the eyes. In the Gilberts, human bait is used. One diver swims to the octopus cave and dances in front of it until the octopus comes out and embraces him. A second diver then swims down and bites the octopus between the eyes, killing it instantly. The brain is located between the creature's eyes and is its most vulnerable spot. The Gilbert Island skin-divers have concluded that the reason an octopus embraces the human bait is not because it is aggressive, but because it is curious. Octopuses will many times approach and feel any new and unusual object with their tentacles. The islanders say that if a diver can breathe long enough and remain still the octopus will eventually release its grip and return to its cave.

Famous French scuba diver, Frederick Dumas tells us that, "Once an octopus is truly frightened, it will respond to anything." Dumas proved this statement by having movies taken of him dancing with an octopus for ten to twenty minutes underwater. "After the waltz," says Jacques Cousteau in his classic, *The Silent World*, "the octopus had a nervous collapse." California scuba divers like Bill Barada and Bill High have gone one step further. They spend weekends wrestling octopuses in their own domain, just for sport. The two 'Bills' aggravate octopuses into a fighting mood by placing a salt solution at the mouth of their caves. Salt irritates the skin of the octopus, causing it to come charging out of its home ready for battle. The divers meet the monsters in combat and swim with them to the surface, where they are either released or chopped up for dinner. Three octopus hunters were arrested at Laguna Beach, California in 1964, when they were caught introducing copper sulfate into the water to aggravate octopuses. The toxic "bluestone" cause the octopuses to scuttle out from their hiding places in an effort to escape. When they came out of hiding, the three offenders speared them. The game warden fined the offenders $150.00 for violating a California code which makes it unlawful to "introduce any material deleterious to fish or plant life into the water."

In Oregon there is an annual Octopus Jamboree, where 40 to 60 scuba divers meet to see how many pounds of octopus they can capture and bring to the surface in a designated amount of time. The diver who collects the most poundage wins and the diver who captures the biggest octopus also gets a prize. Rules of the Jamboree are that octopuses must not be injured in any way, and divers are not allowed to use weapons. After the contest, all captives are returned to the water. The largest one taken from the waters off Seattle by a scuba diver weighed 89 pounds with tentacles eight feet long. The octopus was given to the Seattle Marine Aquarium and is today the largest in captivity. Marineland Of The Pacific has an 80 pounder in captivity, which was brought up from a depth of 360 feet, off Zuma Beach, in southern California.

Some divers capture these octopuses by reaching into their caves and tickling their tentacles. Others report that an octopus will go limp when they rub its hind cloak. By petting this cloak, or mantle which looks like a black cape, the octopus relaxes its grip and is easily captured. Benjamin Franklin once said that vinegar, sprinkled on the mantle of an octopus would make it release its grip. The reason for this reaction in the female octopus may be because her sex organs are located in a cavity directly beneath this mantle.

The male octopus grows a special sperm-bearing attachment on one or more of its tentacles every year. When a male octopus "gives his hand in marriage," he does so literally — detaching one of his arms and giving it to the female. She in turn, keeps the arm with her until it dies. Approximately fifty days later, eggs hatch and by this time, the male octopus has grown back a new arm. When the female lays her eggs, the male comes around again, but this time he's looking for food and the female must chase him away before he gobbles up his own offspring. A female octopus will fight to the death to protect her young. Octopus eggs are called "sea grapes," for they look like clusters of green grapes on a vine. The female hatches approximately 50,000 eggs annually, but because of preying male octopuses and other molesting fish, only a small percentage of baby octopuses reach maturity.

In the nautilus family, the male implants the sperm in the female, and like the octopus, gives the female a special modified arm. The paper thin shell of the female nautilus is utilized as an egg case and when the eggs are ready to hatch, she blows them out of her shell. It is also thought that the female may die immediately after producing her offspring. Divers and scientists have noticed that in many instances, the female nautilus will leave her shell after the babies are hatched. She is not connected to her shell, but once she looses it, she cannot grow another and will eventually perish to predators. Periodically, at various coastal areas around the world, beaches will be littered with empty nautilus shells. In 1967, the outer islands around New Zealand, according to Dr. A. Powell of the Auckland Museum, were strewn with shells. There were also several dead bodies of female nautilus washed ashore. In 1936, the beaches of the Adriatic Sea were similarly infested with nautilus shells.

In December of each year, hundreds of thousands of small, milky-colored squid migrate on a one-way bridal journey to the shallow waters off southern California. Divers have witnessed the matings of this multitude, reporting that the male squids use the two longest of ten tentacles to transfer sperm into mantle cavities of the females. After a very brief courtship, the squids mate and the female swims to the bottom, at a depth of between 30 and 60 feet, to bury her eggs in the sand. After this ceremony, both the male and the female die and the eggs are hatched within thirty-five days. Before hatching, the eggs are kept in natural, finger-like capsules. These transparent cases hold up to 400 eggs. Dr. John McGowan of Scripps Institution of Oceanography has reported seeing a cluster of these egg capsules on the ocean bottom in Monterey Bay, over one quarter of a mile long by 200 yards wide. This life cycle of small squids has apparently repeated for eons, each year off the coast of California. It is also known that giant squid appear off the coast of Newfoundland every 30 years, possibly for the same reason that their smaller counterpart visits Californian waters.

Plagues of octopus and cuttlefish have also erupted from time to time, especially off the coasts of England and France. In 1950, thousands of dead cuttlefish washed ashore in Northern France. Experts claimed that the reason for this mass death was either extreme water temperature change, or the results of a mating cycle. In Northern France the year before, thousands of octopuses littered the beaches and were carted away by farmers for fertilizer. This octopus plague, which invaded England the following year, put many fishermen out of business. The octopuses were eating all the crabs, oysters and muscles and instead of catching lobsters in their pots, lobstermen found octopuses living in them. Similar octopus plagues are recorded off Scotland in 1900 and again in 1930.

Usually the octopus, unlike its cousins the nautilus and squid, does not travel the oceans, but spends its entire life wandering no further than 100 yards or so from its own cave. Divers who visit the same underwater area year after year have found the same octopuses there to greet them every time. A group of California scuba divers who spend much of their time exploring the waters off Catalina Island, made friends with an old octopus that lives in a shallow water cave there. The divers studied its habits and found that after six or seven dives, the octopus would follow them along the bottom, waiting for any tidbits they might stir up as they dug for abalone. The divers also discovered that the old octopus started decorating the entrance of its cave with abalone shells and pretty stones.

One day the divers decided to play a prank on the old octopus. They removed all the shells and stones from its cave entrance and spent hours clearing the underwater area of all the abalone shells they could find. "What will the old boy do now?" they wondered. Their answer came a few days later when they returned to the octopus cave. Unable to find stones or shells to decorate the entrance to its home, the old octopus found a suitable substitute — the cave entrance was now sparkling with stacks of empty beer cans.

The most unusual incident involving an octopus and its acquired possessions occurred in August of 1962. Kenneth Blake of London lost his false teeth while swimming at a beach in Loano, Italy. Kenneth had to return home without his uppers and lowers. A week later, he met a friend in London named George Farrell, who was on his way to Loano for his annual vacation. "I'll keep an eye out for your choppers," said George jokingly. At Loano, a few days later, George happened to be watching a fisherman who had just speared an octopus and was hauling it onto the beach. Clutched in its tentacles was a set of false teeth. George took the teeth from the octopus, and upon his return to London, handed them over to Kenneth Blake. "I bet you won't believe me," said Kenneth, "but the teeth are mine."

What is the octopus? An underwater clown, an aggressive monster, a shy introvert, or could it possibly be the most intelligent creature in the sea? Are octopuses, like human beings, a complexity of characters and personalities? Only time and a continued study of these ugly creatures will tell. We have much to learn about the octopus, and surely in the process we will learn something from him.

The nurse shark is the only shark that can remain on the bottom without swimming to breathe through its gills. Photographer Tzimoulis, it's noted, approached this huge creature from behind.

III
MAN VERSUS SHARK

One of the oldest creatures in the world is the shark. It appeared on the scene before the dinosaur, sometime between 350 to 70 million years ago. Since its inception, the shark has been the undisputed ruler of two-thirds of this earth; and man, who has only been around for about one million years, likes to make claim to the other one-third. Since man first set foot into the sea, his greatest enemy has been the shark. One of the earliest records of man being attacked by a shark is portrayed on an ancient vase, which dates back to 725 B.C. It shows a sailor being swallowed by what appears to be a tiger shark. To my knowledge, the first man to befriend a shark was Italian Maurizio Serra. He wrote a book, "My Friend the Shark," in which he told of his many adventurers with sharks that were not only friendly but showed no signs of aggression. Unfortunately, this great Italian diver never had the opportunity to complete his experiments with "friendly" sharks, for in 1963, he died in the Tyrrhenia Sea, the victim of a shark attack.

The shark didn't receive its name until the sixteenth century. Prior to that time, it was considered just another sea monster. An English sea captain captured one in the late 1500's and displayed it in the market at London, England. During this exhibit, the tough-skinned creature was called a "schurke," a German word meaning "villain." The British soon bastardized the word by pronouncing it "shark." Although the shark has always been man's greatest sea enemy, it wasn't until the mid-twentieth century that we began to learn something about its character, personality and habits. Until that time, all that was heard about these creatures were gruesome stories of attacks and occasional unbelievable reports of items found in the bellies of captured specimens.

One of the strangest reports came from Sydney, Australia, in 1935, when a shark solved a murder in that city. Eight days after a shark had been captured in nets and placed in the Sydney Aquarium, it vomited up a well-preserved, tattooed man's arm. After examining the arm, doctors determined that it had not been separated from the body by the shark's teeth, but had been neatly severed with a knife. The tattoo was easily traced and police soon discovered that the arm belonged to an ex-prize-fighter who had supposedly died in a shipwreck off the Australian coast. Further investigation proved that the pleasure ship had been deliberately wrecked to collect insurance and that the prize-fighter had been murdered before it went down. His body had been jammed into a box and dropped overboard, but since one arm wouldn't fit into the container, the murderers threw it overboard, never, of course, expecting that a shark would swallow it and preserve it as evidence.

Another shark story — even more amazing than the Australian shark sleuth — indirectly caused the British-American War of 1812. On July 3, 1799, the

American brig NANCY, under the command of Thomas Briggs, with a cargo eventually destined for France, put out from Baltimore, Maryland. At the time, England was at war with France, and the British had set up blockades along the American coast, knowing that the Yanks were supporting their old Revolutionary War ally. Briggs carried two packets of shipping orders wrapped in oilskins. One was the official papers showing the actual cargo destination; the other was a substitute forgery, which stated that the cargo was going to a British port. When the NANCY reached the Caribbean Sea, the British patrol boat SPARROW came along side. As the Redcoats boarded the NANCY, Captain Briggs dropped his real orders overboard and showed the British the forged papers. As was the British custom of the time, the NANCY was escorted into Port Royal, Jamaica, and the Yankee skipper forced to go before the British court. Briggs, however, was confident that he would be acquitted and soon be on his way. He concluded that the British could never prove that his orders were false.

Two days later, as Briggs' trial got underway, the British warship, H.M.S. FERRET was cruising off the Caribbean Island of San Domingo. Her skipper, Lt. Michael Fitton, often fished off the stern of his ship, and this day he caught a large shark. With the help of his crew, he hauled the shark aboard and cut open its stomach. Inside the shark was a packet wrapped in oilskin — the original orders of the bark NANCY, showing her true destination to be a French port. Lt. Fitton sailed for Jamaica and arrived at the courthouse in time to present British officials with the NANCY's real papers. Captain Briggs' ship was confiscated by the British and he went to prison. This bizarre episode further strained relations between England and America, and was a major factor leading to the War of 1812. Lt. Fitton sent the shark's jaws to the Museum of the Royal Institute of London, where they were displayed until 1964. With the package, Fitton sent a note which read: "I recommend these jaws for a collar for neutrals to swear through."

Although the digestive juices or acids in a shark's stomach can eat through human bones within minutes and have been known to dissolve a metal fish hook within three days, the shark can, at will, store items in its belly for weeks without digesting them. Thus, on a few rare occasions when a shark is captured and cut open, the results are fascinating and sometimes almost unbelievable. For example, the crew of a merchant ship cruising the South Atlantic captured a 24-foot shark, and when its stomach was cut open, 27 items were found inside including: a pair of tennis shoes, a jar of nails, a flashlight, a large kettle, a cigar box, a carpenter's square, a rubber raincoat, two soft drink bottles, and 27 feet of tar paper. These were all items that had been dropped or thrown overboard from the merchant ship during her Atlantic cruise.

A 20-foot great white shark was captured off Australia a few years ago and its stomach contained one 100 lb. sea lion, eight turtles, and a seven foot shark.

Another white shark netted off Australia had in its stomach; half a ham, a head and forelegs of a bulldog with a rope around its neck, and part of a horse. Hooked in the Pacific off the American coast, another white revealed a fur coat, a sack of coal, an alarm clock, and a dog still wearing its collar. A large shark captured in the Adriatic contained three overcoats and an automobile license plate. Off the Bahama Islands in 1951, a tiger shark was cut open to expose a native's leg and his three-foot tom-tom, still intact. According to the records of A.I.X. in France, fishermen of that seaport once captured a shark, and in its stomach was a decapitated male dressed in a complete suit of armor!

The above seems to bear out the old seaman's saying that "a shark will eat anything," and this of course brings up a question to all men who are in any way connected to the sea: "Will the shark eat me?" In answering that question, ichthyologist J.L.B. Smith of South Africa says, "It depends on how you smell." He believes that some humans possess "a special smell about them that makes them either appetizing or unappetizing to sharks." Dr. Smith's theory is just one of many concerning the feeding habits of sharks and the reasons why they do or do not attack certain humans. Some believe that species of sharks will attack blindly at anything they see moving in the water; especially on the surface waters, which are their feeding grounds. Many marine scientists say that the sight or smell of blood will send sharks into an eating frenzy, and others are quite certain that vibrations attract sharks to their prey.

Probably the one scientist who has experimented more with live sharks than any other man is Dr. Perry Gilbert, professor of Zoology at Cornell University. Most of Dr. Gilbert's tests were conducted at the Lerner Marine Laboratory on Bimini Island, 50 miles off the coast of Miami, Florida. Here, Dr. Gilbert worked with large sharks of varying species to determine how they recognize and attack their victims. He blindfolded sharks, recorded their heart beats and brain waves, and used various types of chemicals and dyes to record their reactions. His conclusions thus far are that most sharks cannot see things in great detail like humans can; but that they do see small changes in light and shadow, and are quick to see any little thing that moves in the water. In murky water or dim light, sharks have eyes like cats and can see much better in this atmosphere than humans and other fish. Sharks are also able to detect minute quantities of certain substances such as blood in seawater. By connecting electrical signal devices to a shark's brain, and then dropping a small quantity of tuna fish juice into the water with the shark, Dr. Gilbert was able to prove without doubt, that the shark smelled the tuna and reacted to it. Then he experimented with other liquids to find out what, if anything, repelled sharks. A substance called "Shark Chaser" was the result. It was made up of copper acetate and a dye additive, and although it did ward off many sharks when dropped into the water, it had no effect on some species. During tests at Brisbane, Australia, sharks actually ate the shark repellent as it was deposited in the water. A second ingredient used in "Shark Chaser" is a dye called nigrosine, which spreads a dark blue cloud over the water. This repellent works well on lemon sharks, but not on tiger sharks. However, some undersea scientists have concluded that sharks definitely dislike the color blue for some unknown reason. In numerous tests, certain species of shark swam rapidly away from any object in the water that was colored blue. Dr. Eugene Clark has experimented with colors and has concluded that sharks are attracted by striped targets. She says that her experiments proved that they preferred vertical rather than horizontal stripes, which may be because many fish have vertical stripes. Dr. Clark also discovered that lemon sharks will swim swiftly towards a yellow colored target, then stop short before touching it, and sometimes go into convulsions. She also found that many sharks are disturbed by quick color changes. During her tests at the Lerner Laboratory, some sharks died when the target changed color. Dr. Clark also concluded that female sharks learn faster than male sharks.

The office of Naval Research is presently sponsoring a study to provide a new shark repellent and thus far, from this study, scientists have utilized with some success the cloudy substance emitted by the sea cucumber. The sea cucumber is a long, black marine animal found on the ocean bottom that resembles a pickle. When molested, it secretes a substance which causes its enemies to retreat. It is hoped that this same substance may be commercially produced and used as an effective shark repellent.

Another shark expert is Professor David H. Davies, of the Oceanographic Research Institute, Durban, South Africa. He has been studying the reactions of different species of sharks to air bubble curtains. In the Durban experimentation tank, a bubble screen separated the sharks at one end of the tank and food at the other. When the food was not there, most sharks would not swim through the barrier; however, with the temptation of food present, very few species would not swim through the bubbles. Therefore, bubble curtains are a disappointment in trying to keep sharks away from beaches. New Jersey officials found this out the hard way. A $400,000 bubble curtain was erected off the New Jersey coast a few years ago and it worked for only ten minutes. It was discovered that lemon sharks weren't frightened of the bubbles at all; and although tiger sharks hesitated at first, they soon passed freely back and forth through the screen, apparently enjoying their bubble bath.

Professor Davies is also experimenting with electrical fields to repel sharks. He has thus far discovered that sharks react violently to electrical shocks that do not effect humans. Also, that larger sharks are more sensitive to an electrical shock than smaller ones. At the University of Miami's Institute of Marine Science, electrodes were attached near the heart of captive sharks to determine whether or not certain wave lengths attract or repel them. Using recordings of the sounds emitted by hooked and wounded fish, Dr. Warren Wisby found that sharks are attracted to the sounds of dying fish and will be on the scene within seconds. It is possible that some sharks can hear a fish in distress up to two or three miles away. The Shark Research Society of Sydney, Australia and Dr. Eugene Agalides of GD/Electronics, Rochester, New York, are also trying to discover a single electric wave form that will repel sharks. "The problem is that a wave form common to all species of sharks must be found," says Dr. Agalides, "and it also must be one that will be effective under various sea conditions." Only then will the world have an effective shark repellent.

The American Navy has come up with a five-foot plastic bag with an inflatable ring, inside of which a man, supported by a life-jacket, can float and be protected. Tests have proved, thus far, that most sharks avoid the floating bag with the man inside — probably because the smell of the person does not reach the shark through the plastic.

Therefore, one can conclude from the many various experiments that sharks are unpredictable, and that although one specie may react favorably to one stimuli, another type of shark will reject it. Sharks have an extraordinary sense of smell and like hound dogs following a scent, they are able to detect the blood and skin secretions of a dying fish hundreds of yards away. Most scientists believe that sharks smell or taste their food through their tough skin, and that this is the reason why they usually bump or nudge their prey before attacking it.

The shark is also attracted by various types of underwater explosions. Internal canals running from its small brain along both sides of its body give the shark the pressure perception. The sounds of depth charges, torpedoes hitting their mark, and the exploding heads of spear guns quickly bring sharks to the scene. Even the dropping of a nose-cone into the sea from outer space attracts sharks. Sonar signals from a partially submerged spacecraft travel five times faster underwater than they do in air. When Navy frogmen were assigned to rescue astronauts from a floating nosecone, one diver watched for sharks, as the others proceeded with rescue duties. During the first astronaut rescue missions, Navy frogmen complained about being nudged by large sharks.

Most shark attacks occur in shallow water — sometimes only two feet deep, and usually when the water is murky. Also, from reading the many shark attack reports, it seems that the smaller sharks are the more aggressive. However, of the 300 or so different species of sharks in the sea, only 25 are known to be dangerous to man. These man-eaters usually frequent the tropics where the temperature of the water is 70 degrees or warmer.

The most dangerous sharks are the mako and white. The average length of the mako is 13 feet. It is very aggressive and fast; can leap 20 feet or more out of the water and has been known to attack boats. For its size, the mako is probably the toughest creature in the sea. Captain Art Wills of the charter boat SEA QUEEN, out of Florida, can attest to the power of the mako probably better

A South African biologist inspects a Mako shark after it ate one man and mauled another, below.
Photos by Michael Hely.

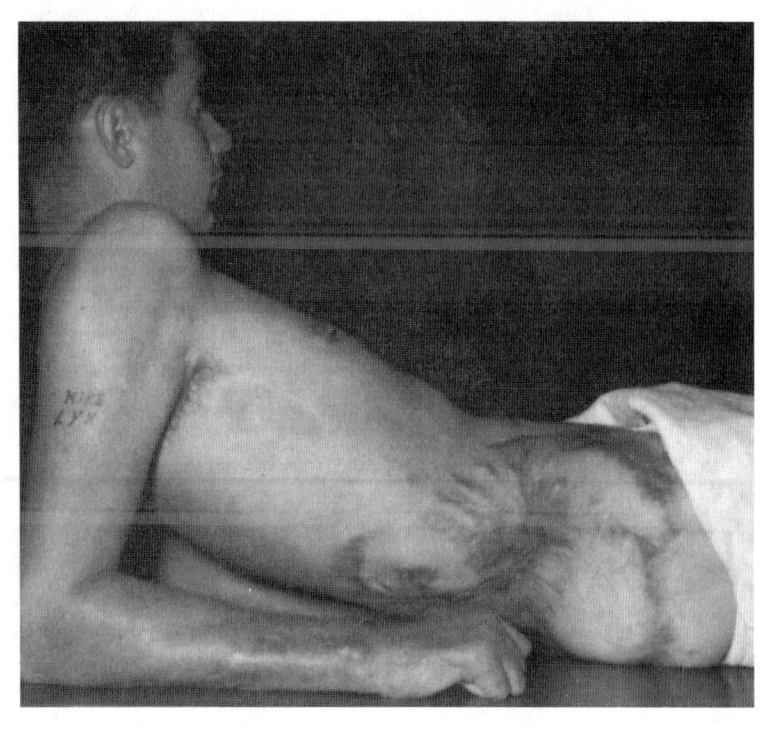

than anyone else. He snagged a 400 pounder on a line and battled it for two hours before he could haul it aboard. It was still very lively on deck — even after the captain and crew clubbed it over 100 times and stabbed it in the head with an ice pick 46 times. It then snapped the ropes that tied it down and leaped overboard. With the hook still in its mouth, it took one hour to bring it aboard again. The captain then cut out its brain with a knife and the crew sat on its quivering body all the way back to port.

Even the U.S. Navy has fought losing battles with makos. Recently, on the island of Guam, two seamen tried to capture a 600-pounder that they saw swimming near the coast. They rigged a winch to their Jeep and baited a hook with fifteen pounds of beef, which they attached to a thick wire line. Dropping the hook off a nearby reef, they jumped into the Jeep to await the battle. When the first tug was felt, the boys raced the Jeep inland, but quickly found themselves being forced backward. They braked the Jeep, but that didn't help either. Finally, they jumped out of the vehicle and watched it being towed under the waves. Today, somewhere in the depths off Guam, there is a large mako shark leading a Jeep along the ocean bottom.

Whalers have reported catching makos, disemboweling them, and throwing them back into the water, only to have them swim back to attack a harpooned whale. There was also an incident where a mako's head was chopped off and the severed head, when picked up by a sailor, slammed it jaws, biting off the sailor's finger.

The white, or great white shark, which gained world wide notoriety in the movie "Jaws," is very voracious and will attack bathers and boats sometimes without being provoked. It is found in every ocean, but is not common anywhere. Like most sharks, its six rows of teeth are razor-sharp. The white, and its cousin the probeagle or mackerel shark, can grow to 40-feet in length and weigh five tons or more. The white-tipped shark, with distinctive white markings on the tip of its pectoral and dorsal fins, is also a man-eater.

Frank Mundus hooked and reeled in a Great White Shark off Montauk, New York, on August 6, 1986. It took him two hours to land the monster that was 15' 8" long and weighed 3,450 pounds — it's the largest white shark thusfar ever caught with a rod and reel. Usually it's the Great White that catches man, and seven years after the Montauk catch, another record was set off the shores of Sydney, Australia, where whites often frequent. John Ford, on his honeymoon, was attacked and killed by a great white while swimming on June 10, 1993 — five days earlier, another man was killed north of Sydney by another great white shark.

Two other dangerous species are the dusky brown and the bull shark. The dusky or brown, which in Africa is called the Zambezi or "shovelnose," will make unprovoked attacks, as will the blunt-nosed bull shark, and both swim in fresh water as well as salt. The bull and dusky are related to the Lake Nicaragua fresh water shark. It is believed that this landlocked lake in Central America was once part of the sea, which was closed off by a volcanic eruption and slowly turned to fresh water. The sharks of Lake Nicaragua are extremely dangerous. Several years ago, a young girl was attacked by a bull shark in the Caloosahatchee River, above Fort Myers, Florida; and recently, an angel shark was caught far up Michigan's St. Claire River. The bull has been known to ascend the rivers of Florida and Louisiana for 100 miles or farther. Zambezi sharks also travel rivers and have been seen 300 miles inland from the sea. A few years ago, Zambezi sharks attacked and devoured an elephant in a river at Kenya, East Africa.

The hammerhead shark with its T-shaped head, and the long snouted tiger shark are dangerous to man also. In the stomachs of scavenging tiger sharks such items as whole crocodiles, seals, goats, pigs and tin cans have been found. The tiger is a cannibal even before birth. The first baby tiger to hatch waits outside the egg cases of his siblings, and when they emerge, he eats them. Thus, a pregnant tiger shark may produce many eggs, but usually only one off-spring results from a multiple birth. Most sharks give birth to live young which emerge six to sixty at one time.

The wolfish-looking lemon shark of the Caribbean and Gulf of Mexico is not to be trusted either. Although the lemon shark appears to have a small mouth, when its jaws unlock and open up, it becomes almost completely mouth.

The blue shark, which is recognized by its brilliant blue back and pure white belly, likes to travel in schools and follows ships to feed on the garbage and debris thrown overboard. Fishermen have reported seeing blues up to 25 feet long, weighing close to a ton. The blue has recently become a popular game fish, offering a splendid battle for the sports fisherman. Off Nags Head, North Carolina, Bob Keller caught the biggest blue ever on a hook and line. It was 11 feet long, weighed 610 pounds, and it took Keller 11/2 hours to capture it. A second record blue, 11-feet 6-inches long and weighing 410 pounds, was hooked off Rockport, Massachusetts — but larger blue sharks have been caught in fishing nets.

Another shark, which some consider dangerous and others debate, is the nurse shark. The nurse, with its two whisker-like barbells hanging from its mouth, is much feared along the coast of Australia, but not feared at all in the Mediterranean Sea. It may be concluded, however, that the nurse shark will bite when provoked no matter where it makes its home. It has tiny teeth, but very powerful jaws, grows to a length of 14-feet, and is one of the only sharks that can rest on the sea bottom, pumping water through its gills. All other types of sharks, except some sand sharks, will sink to the bottom if they stop swimming — they must swim continuously to "breathe," forcing water over their gills. If a shark on a line is towed too fast in water, it will drown.

The thresher shark isn't a man-eater, but its long tail is used like a sickle to kill other fish, and has, occasionally, knocked fishermen off rocks and out of boats, leaving them with nasty scars. The spiny sand shark isn't considered a man-eater either, but there is a stinger at the forward tip of its dorsal fin that contains a venom that, when injected into humans, this venom can cause death.

The sand shark or dogfish, cousin of the spiny sand shark, is not dangerous; yet it is one of the most hated sharks in the world. Atlantic coast fishermen have estimated that the annual damage to other fish and fishing gear by sand sharks is upwards of $5 million. In Massachusetts alone, sand sharks cost fishermen over $400,000 every year. Fishermen have suggested that the government inoculate sand sharks with a fatal disease to get rid of them. In large schools, sand sharks make annual trips along the Atlantic coast traveling some 2,500 miles; and when they visit the fishing grounds, all other fish disappear. In New England, some fishermen blame the depletion of haddock on sand sharks. Over 27 million of them are caught by fishermen off the New England coast every year, and not by choice — the sharks simply get tangled in the nets and are hauled aboard. Approximately 60,000 of these are sold to American colleges and universities for dissection by biology and anatomy students.

The sand shark, which grows to a maximum length of four feet, lives in the shallows but has been known to swim in depths up to 3,600 feet. Its huge liver contains rich fish oils sold by some European fishermen commercially. Also, in Europe and only recently in America, sand sharks are sold as food. In England, it is often served as a famous "fish and chips" and in Japan, sand shark sausages are peddled at the baseball games and eaten in a roll, much like the American hot dog. It is interesting to note that although the sea seems to be over-populated with sand sharks, the female of the species gives birth only once every other year.

Another shark that has a high content of oil in its liver is the Greenland or Arctic shark. This cold water shark is very slow moving and docile. Off Greenland, fishermen easily catch it through the ice. Arctic sharks grow to a length of 20 feet and, although seemingly lazy and non-aggressive, one was caught recently which contained the remains of a full-grown reindeer in its stomach.

A new species of shark was recently discovered off Nauri, New Zealand, at a depth of 1,400 feet. These deep water creatures live in perpetual darkness and were photographed when television cameras and lights were lowered into the depths in an attempt to discover new fish life. Two eight foot sharks, previously unknown to zoologists, swam before the cameras, and after reviewing the footage, it was concluded that these sharks have no eyes and because of their blindness, were unaffected by the powerful TV lights.

The two largest members of the shark family are completely harmless, and if provoked or attacked, will swim away. The whale shark is not only the biggest shark, but is the biggest fish in the underwater world. It averages 50 feet in length and weighs several tons. The eggs of a whale shark are over one-foot long. In 1912, Charles Thompson caught the biggest whale shark ever captured in American waters, when he harpooned it off the coast of Knight's Key, Florida. It took him eight hours to bring the 30 foot, 26,584 pound creature ashore.

The whale shark feeds on plankton and other minute sea animals and probably would choke trying to swallow anything bigger than a golf ball. The basking shark also feeds on plankton, and although it reaches a maximum length of 45 feet and is gruesome in appearance, it too is harmless. Unlike other sharks having tough sandpaper-like skin, basking and whale sharks have smooth, mucous-like skin.

A few years ago, the California Department of Fish and Game, spied six divers at La Jolla hitching rides on about 50 basking sharks swimming off the coast. The divers would wait for the 20 foot long creatures to swim by and they would grab their tails for a dizzy up-and-down ride. When the divers returned to shore, officials of the Department gave them a good tongue-lashing for molesting the sharks. Recently, at California's Catalina Island, a rare yet harmless shark called "Megamouth" was hauled up from the deep. It was only the second ever to be captured in the world. The first Megamouth was hauled ashore at Hawaii in 1976, which caused a great sensation, for no one was aware that the creature even existed. The large-mouthed shark netted off Catalina was 14 feet in length and weighed over a ton, with a mouth that could easily encompass the body of a man — possibly even two men at once, but it's a plankton eater and can't swallow anything bigger than a pencil.

Many divers who frequent shark infested waters carry a stick or pole, sometimes with a spike at the end of it, to push back curious sharks. Some carry spears with explosive heads in them, which they use to tap the shark on the head and blow out its brain. Others descend in shark cages and swim close to the cage in case they have to rush inside to avoid an attack.

Divers who have been attacked by sharks, or have witnessed attacks on buddy divers, report many similarities as to the approach, physical behavior, and attitude of the attacker. Before approaching the victim to take a bite, a shark usually swims in jerky, erratic movements, with its head moving back and forth like its tail. Its pectoral fins slant down and it tilts its nose slightly upwards; it seems to hunch its back first, and then dart out at the victim with lightening speed. Some say the eyes of sharks, especially the hammerhead, turn flame red before an attack.

A shark does not turn upside down — as once was suspected — before it attacks, but its dorsal fins almost never appear on the surface as it attacks. It will usually strike out at anything on the surface waters, and will more than likely be attracted to fluttery or irregular motions, like those of a hooked or speared fish.

"It was like being hit by a train," said diver Henri Bource of Melbourne, Australia, after a 14 foot white-pointer shark bit off his leg. Bource was skin-diving, playing with wild seals on the surface off Port Fairy, when the shark "gripped my leg like a vise and dragged me underwater. I'm sure I would have drowned if my leg had not come away in the shark's mouth." Bource was hauled aboard a boat by fellow divers. Although it took the boat 1 1/2 hours to reach shore and a hospital, the 25 year old diver was saved, and while in the hospital he said that he would be skin-diving again, "as soon as I am physically fit."

Australian spear fishing champion, Brian Rodgers, had a similar horrifying experience in March, 1961. He was diving in a spear fishing competition off the coast of Adelaide, South Australia. Rodgers was swimming one-half mile from land, towing about fifty pounds of fish that he had speared, when the shark struck. "The first warning I had of the shark was when my body convulsed with a stifled deep scream, as the shark's teeth sunk into my left leg," said Rodgers. "...I quickly swung to my left side and was horrified to see the jaws of a huge white-pointer about 12 feet long clamped over my leg. My immediate reaction was to get my thumb into its eye, but as I lunged my left hand toward it, the jaws must have released the grip on my leg...and my outstretched hand went down its throat. I felt the sharp teeth tear at my arm and I quickly pulled it back. How close I came to losing my left hand I will never know." Rodgers then managed to aim his spear gun and fire into the shark's head. It trembled in pain from the impact and quickly retreated. Rodgers applied a tourniquet to his leg and held the pressure point under his left arm to arrest the bleeding there. He ditched his fish and swam the mile or more distance to shore. Both his arm and leg were saved, but they required many stitches to close the wounds.

There was another attack on a diver during a spear fishing contest off Adelaide, Australia in December, 1963. Rodney Fox was free diving almost a mile off-shore at a depth of 40 feet. He was about to shoot a 20 pound fish with his spear gun, when there was "a tremendous force on my left side that heaved me through the water." The impact also knocked the spear gun out of his hand. Like Rodgers, his first thought was to gouge out the shark's eyes, and he too found his arm deep in the shark's mouth. "I felt pain such as I had never imagined," Fox later reported. Wrenching his arm loose, he headed for the surface and air. When Fox finally broke the surface, he saw the shark's dorsal fin racing towards him. However, the shark got tangled in the rope that was attached to Fox's surface float. This apparently frightened the creature and it swam off, leaving Fox in a pool of blood — his rib cage, lungs, and upper stomach exposed to the salt water. Within minutes, a boat with his fellow divers aboard was on the scene. Today, a badly scarred yet happy-to-be-alive Rodney Fox still goes skin-diving in the deep shark-infested waters off Australia.

Another Australian spear fisherman (wishing to remain anonymous) was recently attacked by a wobbegong shark off Rottnest Island. The usually sluggish and harmless wobbegong clamped onto the diver's arm. Quickly swimming to the aid of his wounded friend, a buddy diver pried the shark's jaws away with a knife. As the diver attempted to climb into his boat, the wobbegong took a good bite out of the seat of his pants. Divers hauled the victim and shark aboard the boat, and after some difficulty, pried the shark from its coveted dinner.

A spear fishing native of the Tuamotus Islands experienced an attack and an undesired ride on a shark. When the shark made its first attack, the native, who was swimming in shallow water, jumped onto its back to avoid being bitten. Terrified, he held onto the creature's dorsal fin for dear life. The shark rushed to the surface in an attempt to loose its rider; it leaped into the air and accidentally landed on a small island reef. The native quickly jumped off the shark, surprised to find himself on dry land. As the shark tried to wriggle its way back into the water, the diver decided to take revenge. Walking over to the struggling creature, he attempted to punch it in the nose; the shark opened its mouth and in a flash, bit off the native's hand.

Diver Ernest Grover of Panama City, Florida, didn't realize he was being attacked either until his head was inside the shark's mouth. He was underwater, searching for fish, when suddenly the shark was upon him. With his face and one arm inside the shark's mouth, Grover fought for his life and managed to cut the shark's throat. The shark loosened his grip, and the bleeding diver swam to shore. Mr. Grover recovered — but has many teeth scars on his head as a result of his battle.

Skin-diver Edward Dawkins, a hospital intern at Balboa, Canal Zone, also received deep lacerations of the scalp and face when a large shark tried to swallow him whole. Dawkins was swimming in shallow murky water, attempting to dislodge a fish from his spear gun when the shark struck. He managed to escape by punching at the shark's belly. At the hospital, over 100 stitches were required to seal the wounds.

The Farallon Islands, 30 miles off San Francisco, California, was the scene of another brutal attack on a diver in January of 1964. John Rochette was spear fishing for cod with members of his diving club, when a 25-foot white shark was spotted. Many of the divers quickly scrambled aboard their boat, while others sank quietly to the bottom until the shark had passed. Rochette, however, did not have time to escape; the shark slammed into his legs. Observing from the boat, diver Jack Bolger jumped back into the water and swam to Rochette's side. Keeping the shark away by jabbing it with a spear, Bolger carried the victim 150-feet back to the boat. Rochette was rushed to the mainland where he underwent seven blood transfusions. Pieces of the shark's teeth were found embedded in his leg.

Shirley O'Neill and Albert Kogler, both aged 18, were swimming at Baker's Beach outside San Francisco's Golden Gate, when Shirley heard Albert scream. She turned and saw "a big gray thing flop up in the air." He screamed again, "It's a shark, get out of here!" But Shirley didn't heed his warning; instead, she swam towards him, and dragged Albert some 50-yards to shore. He was badly mauled and died 2 1/2 hours later. President John F. Kennedy awarded Miss O'Neill the Young American Medal for Bravery.

The coveted George Medal was awarded to diver Jostaki Tunisau, of Naviti Island in the Fijian Group, for trying to save a shark attack victim. A local diver was attacked by a seven-foot tiger shark and Jostaki swam to his aide. He carried his mauled companion on his back for almost an hour before he reached shore, having to dive continuously to make the shark retreat. Despite his efforts, Jostaki's friend died.

Ten-year-old Steve Samples was floating along in a rubber raft off Palm Beach, Florida, when the raft was suddenly lifted out of the water. It was the summer of 1969, and there had been three shark attacks off Palm Beach the previous year. Douglas Fletcher, a vacationing Canadian bank official, was standing on the beach and saw Steven tumble off the raft; then he spotted the shark's tail and the pool of blood. Jumping into the water, he surfaced near the raft, clamped a hand over the boy's left elbow which was spurting blood, and swam back to shore with him. Other witnesses said the boy had been attacked by more than one shark and was dragged off the raft. When Steven regained consciousness, he said, "There were millions of them!" Steven survived, but it took 1,000 stitches to seal his wounds.

On Christmas Day, Ronald DeWet of South Africa, who had been swimming off the deserted Natal Coast all day, returned to waist deep water to wash the sand from his bathing suit. A Zambezi shark came up behind him and lifted him out of the water. As Ronald was being dragged under, he gouged at the shark's eyes. Friends on the beach ran to his aid and dragged him ashore as the shark circled. After rescuing him, they found that his left foot was gone, and later, his leg had to be amputated.

Friends of Robert Pomperin witnessed a more horrible sight in 1959. They saw their fellow diver, who was hunting for abalone off La Jolla, California, eaten alive by a large white shark. Before his fellow divers could even attempt to save him, the shark approached Pomperin from the rear and swam away with him in its mouth.

Also off California, seven years earlier, a 17-year-old boy floating in an inflated tire tube was attacked. Five men swam to his aid, and started towing the tube with the wounded boy in it to shore, but the shark kept slipping through the rescuers to attack the boy. The shark never attempted to bite the five men, but before they reached shore, it bit the boy over six times and finally killed him.

There have also been incidents of mass shark attacks where schools of the frenzied creatures attacked shipwrecked victims unmercifully. One such slaughter took place in the South Atlantic on December 7, 1941, the day Pearl Harbor was attacked. A British cruiser was torpedoed by a German U-boat and sank within minutes. Survivors clung to life rafts in the open sea, but then the sharks began their attack, tearing holes into life rafts with their teeth, and pulling under swimming seamen. The few rafts that remained afloat were followed for five days by the sharks, being attacked continuously. Men in the rafts had to beat them off with paddles. Only 170 of the cruiser's 450-man crew survived; most of those who died were victims of sharks.

One of the greatest shark massacres took place off the coast of Zululand, South Africa, on November 28, 1942, when the British steamship NOVA SCOTIA was torpedoed and sank. Aboard the NOVA SCOTIA were 765 Italian prisoners of war and 134 South African soldiers. The torpedo explosion killed only a few men, but the sharks devoured hundreds. Rafts were swamped by sharks and any bodies found floating after the sinking were without legs. Those who survived reported that over 600 men were eaten by the ruthless sharks, and only 192 men lived through the mass shark attack.

Some who survived shipwrecks and shark attacks have reported that remaining in a pool of oil slick helped to ward off the sharks. Apparently, even when in a frenzy, sharks don't like to swim through oil. In the Bahama Islands, natives often rub oil over their bodies before venturing into shark-infested waters. On the island of Nivafoou in the South Pacific, mail is delivered to the coast via steamers, then sealed in tin cans and brought to shore by swimming natives. Nivafoou is probably the only place in the world where the postman is not molested by dogs, but is often chased and bitten by sharks. Native postmen have tried covering their bodies with various oils to protect themselves from shark attacks, but even with this oil coating, the mail doesn't always get through.

Off America's East Coast, the cold North Atlantic, only 22 unprovoked shark attacks have been recorded in the last 100 years, with just nine of these resulting in fatalities. Five were victims of the white shark and four were supposedly killed by the harmless sand shark. Yet, in these same waters, from the tip of

Cape Hatteras to the Canadian border, as many as 800,000 sharks have been caught by fishermen and skin-divers within one single year. Also, according to the U.S. Bureau of Commercial Fisheries, 27 million sand sharks have been caught by commercial fishermen off the Massachusetts coast in one year. The first fatal shark attack on record in American waters was off Long Island, New York, in 1815, by a hammerhead shark.

There were 36 recorded shark attacks in the world in 1960, with 13 deaths resulting — three of them in the United States. Thirty years later, there were 12 shark attacks recorded in the United States; none were fatal. In 1991, there were 28 attacks in the United States — two resulting in death; and that same year, 137 people were attacked by sharks throughout the world, and 48 of them died. From 1960 to 1993, the average number of people killed by sharks each year in the entire world was ten; and during that same period, an average of 16 were struck by lightening, and 17 died from bumble bee stings. Within the last few years, as more and more people venture into the sea for recreation and sport, the incidents of shark attacks has quadrupled. Today, the average number of people killed by sharks each year is 40, and according to reports of the Oceanographic Research Institute of Durban, South Africa, 51% of shark attack victims die.

The two countries where shark attack incidence is greatest are Australia and South Africa, with the United States third on the list. In Durban, South Africa, there were 35 shark attacks on bathers from 1980 to 1990. Even after loose-hanging nets, called shark mesh, were placed in the water around the busiest beaches of South Africa, there were 21 attacks within six years. One of the victims was Errol Fouvie, age 15, of Johannesburg. He was swimming forty yards from shore, in a bathing area protected by offshore nets, when he felt a nudge in the buttocks and was lifted out of the water. The water was only ten-feet deep, and he managed to escape to the beach.

Shark meshing was introduced at the beaches of Sydney, Australia in 1937, and within the first seven weeks, 315 sharks were found strangled to death in the nets. In 1938, the nets encompassing the beaches of Sydney meshed 1,500 sharks, half of them man-eaters. Today, all the major beaches of Australia are protected with shark meshing. The nets are set 100 to 200 yards offshore, parallel to the beaches, and are picked up and reset every few days. Although the nets are meant to repel or dissuade sharks, many of the bold creatures try to swim through them and become entangled. The snared sharks die quickly, for they must continuously move in the water to live. The Sydney nets entangle approximately 100 sharks a year, and the entire meshing operation throughout Australia captures an average of 1,000 sharks per year. In the last two years, not one shark has been sighted inside the nets. Sydney harbor officials are thinking of using an electronic device to lure more sharks, and possibly double the number caught in the mesh nets each year. Australian authorities feel that the nets have been very effective; they believe that one reason fewer sharks are caught in the mesh nets each year is because the dead sharks emit an odor which may be repulsive to the others, forcing them away from the beaches. One thing that the nets do not do though, is protect skin and scuba divers who hunt for fish and shipwrecks outside the protected beaches. However, many of these daring Ausie divers make a sport of searching out and killing sharks.

Sydney diver Barry May, spends much of his time hunting sharks with a spear gun and recently Barry met a 10-footer that was more than a match for him. After shooting the big white-pointer, it started towing him through the water and down to a depth of 90-feet. Then the shark turned on the diver, but luckily for Barry, it got tangled in the line connecting the spear to the gun. Even with the shark almost nose-to-nose with him, Barry wouldn't drop the gun which he had just purchased. He tried to tow the entangled shark to the surface, but the shark kept swimming deeper. Finally, the shark worked itself loose and Barry May raced to the surface, still holding his new spear gun.

Ben Cropp from Sydney is another shark killer. He has invented an underwater shotgun to hunt and kill the man-eaters. The pop-gun, as he calls it, is nothing more than an eight-foot hand spear propelled by a rubber sling, with a twelve gauge shotgun shell attached to its spear head. The gun is pressed to the head or spinal column of the shark and explodes on impact, killing the shark instantly. Ben and a female partner, Van Leman, killed eight sharks using the shotgun during their first one hour dive. Van is probably the first woman to kill a man-eating shark.

Surfers have to be extremely careful and always on the lookout for sharks, for they are bold creatures who have no fear of breaking waves, and often search the surf for playful seals. Daredevil diver Jordan Klein actually goes surfing and water-skiing to look for and kill sharks. He carries a ten-foot harpoon with him and is usually towed behind a boat that travels about 20-miles per hour. Once he spies a shark, he releases the tow rope and thrusts the spear into the shark, using both hands. Mr. Klein says he is not afraid of other sharks being attracted to the scene, for "the noise of the boat's motor scares them off." Jordan Klein has harpooned and killed 55 sharks from a surfboard and water skis. This technique of killing off the shark population is, of course, not recommended. There have been others who tried to deplete the shark menace using simpler methods and failed.

In Helston, England, three fishermen tried to do away with a large shark by strapping explosives to its dorsal fins. They managed to drop the charge from their boat onto the shark's back. The shark quickly swam away and the fishermen awaited the explosion, but to their horror, the shark immediately returned and swam under their boat — the explosion sank their boat. Fortunately, during their swim back to shore they were not molested by sharks.

Great White Shark

Whale Shark

Thresher Shark

Dusky Shark

Hammerhead Shark

Sand Shark

Reef Shark

Tiger Shark

Shark fisherman Mike Burke of the Florida Keys is not usually an impatient man, but after snagging a 15-foot shark on his line and battling the creature for over an hour, he was exhausted and angry. Mr. Burke managed to get the shark to the pier from which he was fishing; but when it kept thrashing, still full of life, he drew a pistol from his belt and shot at the creature, hoping to terminate the battle. The shark jerked away as the shot was fired and the bullet went through Mr. Burke's leg. He crawled away for help as the shark slipped back into the sea.

Another Florida Keys man who once hunted sharks was senior citizen Paul Chotteau; and he would put them to good use after he caught them. Mr. Chotteau invented an unsinkable craft with pontoons that uses "shark power" to tow it through the water. He harnessed the captured creatures between the two pontoons of his boat and claimed that they made wonderful motors, except that sometimes they decide to swim straight down. His boat, however, had been built to withstand a downward tug of eighteen thousand pounds. Mr. Chotteau's dream was to travel 114 miles from the Keys to Bimini Island in his shark-powered boat, but he never could capture a tough 15-foot shark that he felt was needed to withstand the long trip. Mr. Chotteau recently died, his dream unfulfilled.

One reason for the over-population of sharks in the sea is that unlike the whale, whose numbers have dwindled greatly over the past two centuries, man has found no real commercial value for this tough-skinned creature. Some commercial fishermen hunt the mako; its flesh, when prepared properly, tastes somewhat like swordfish. Extreme care must be taken, however, in the preparation of shark meat for food, as its meat is rich in urea, a toxic ammonia, and it decomposes faster than most other meats. On America's West Coast, and in Central and South America, the thresher shark, blue shark, leopard, and bonito sharks are sold and eaten as food. The soupfin shark of the Mid and Far East, has a high gelatin content, and in the Orient, its fins are cut off, dried and held in high esteem as a delicious food. The soupfin shark is also commercially exploited in South Africa for its liver oil. In many parts of the world, shark flesh is sold as a high protein pet food, but the shark's liver should never be eaten by man or animal as it contains such rich vitamin concentrations that it causes serious ill effects. Man discovered shark's liver to be rich in vitamin A during the 1940's. American and European fishermen then caught and sold sharks in great quantities, and for a few years it appeared that sharks might be of some value to mankind. Other simpler methods for acquiring vitamin A were eventually discovered, and the shark was once again unmolested by commercial fishermen.

For years, many fishermen in the West Indies have used shark oil to forecast the weather. The oil, which is extracted from the shark's liver, is kept in a bottle and produces a cloudy appearance when a storm is approaching; sometimes

24 hours before the storm arrives. Apparently the sterols contained in the oil are sensitive to temperature changes.

Also, in ancient times, the Chinese used shark skin as grips on the handles of their swords, for no matter how much sweat and blood splattered on the handle during battle, the grip would never get slippery, and the warrior could clutch it firmly. Shark's skin is covered with "denticles," or small teeth, which makes it tough and durable. In many parts of the world it is still used as sandpaper, but it wasn't until 1920, when a Dane named Brodo Bendixen found a method for tanning shark hides, that it became popular in the leather industry. This hide is called "shargreen" and is the toughest leather in the world.

A serum called "aqualine" is also taken from sharks and is used in the research evaluation and determination of cholesterol content in humans. Shark corneas are also being used in eye transplant experiments, for the shark — especially small sand sharks — have corneas that do not swell in water, as do those of other animals. Probably the most intriguing experiments with sharks, which may make these loathsome creatures more valuable than gold in the near future, is the discovery of "restiform." This rich fluid is produced from shark livers, and has thus far helped to regress cancer in animals. If "restiform" becomes a positive cure for cancer, the shark will become the most sought after creature in the sea. Yet, as important as the shark may become to science and possibly to help feed the world's starving millions, this dangerous creature is a scavenger, and if we should deplete the shark population, the oceans of the world could become seriously polluted.

Nose pointed down and dorsal fin arched, means that this shark prowling Florida waters is about to attack. Photographer Paul Tzimoulis says it was about eleven feet long. He sank into an underwater cave and remaind there until the creature left the area.

IV
FISHING FOR FOOD AND MEDICINE

Since the day Adam bit into the apple and found a worm, fishing has become one of man's favorite past times and has also developed into big business for many of the world's seacoast communities. A worm dangling from a hook and line has been the favored way to catch fish for centuries, as has the use of a hand spear and net. Another accepted method since ancient times has been the use of Indian weirs that trap schools of fish in a maze of mesh from tree branches. There are also a few antiquated, yet unique and effective ways of catching fish that are still used today. The Malayans, for example, fish with their ears, the Venezuelans use live horses for fish bait and the natives of Tongo fish with their teeth.

Within the last fifty years or so, scientists have discovered that certain species of fish make distinctive and sometimes very loud sounds in the sea. The herring emits a shrill whistle, the cod grunts like a pig, the mackerel makes a slight chirping sound and the shrimp, by snapping its tail, makes a sound like the cracking of a whip. The natives of Malaya however, knew about fish noises hundreds of years before the scientists found out. Malayans had always fished with their heads underwater, listening for sounds of the fish they wanted to catch. When they heard the proper sound, they would drop their nets and were always quite successful in bringing up the fish they desired. In Venezuela, the electric eel is considered a delicacy. To catch these dangerous creatures, the natives drive horses into the water to absorb the eels' initial shocks. Then they scoop up the exhausted eels in their nets. The natives of Tonga, in the Cannibal Islands, spear fish from small boats, but the second a fish is brought aboard, the fishermen bites it in the spine. This causes paralysis and stops the fish from struggling.

Fishermen of the Mediterranean often use cotton balls for bait. They toss hundreds of the little balls into the sea and as the fish surface to investigate the white objects, the fishermen spear them. In the Caribbean Sea, West Indian natives use poison leaves of the dogwood tree to catch fish. Natives crush the leaves and drop them into tidal pools. When the fish absorb the toxic chemicals they float to the surface where the natives are waiting to scoop them up. This method of fishing is illegal in most of the West Indian islands, but is still practiced extensively.

American fishermen have also concocted some strange yet workable fishing techniques. One effective trick passed on to Oklahoma and Kansas fishermen by American Indians is to capture catfish by tickling them. The fisherman must first locate his prey by walking a stream or river bank. Catfish often live in small caves just below the water surface. When one is spotted, the fisherman reaches into the cave and tickles it on the head. This persuades the catfish to come out of hiding and then the fisherman can grab it with both hands and land it.

Even in the North Atlantic near Boston, where over 50% of all the fish caught in America are netted, there are fishermen who never use a hook, net or spear, nor do they ever set foot in a boat. These fishermen walk the beaches with peach baskets looking for whiting, a thin silvery fish which is also known as silver hake. The agile whiting chases sand eels into shallow water and more often than not, it gets so involved in the pursuit that it gets stranded on wet sand. It then waits until another wave washes it back into the sea. New England fishermen find it quite lucrative to patrol the beaches with baskets and catch the stranded whitings as they wait for that second wave. Wave dodging fishermen who follow schools of whiting from beach to beach capture them by the bushel.

Although these unusual fishing methods do bring successful results, most fishermen today rely on techniques that have been handed down from father to son for generations. Yet, fishermen know very little about the habits of their quarry or about the environment in which they live. Even when new and more effective fishing techniques are discovered and introduced, tradition oriented fishermen often will not accept them.

Ichthyologists from Woods Hole Oceanographic Institute had a difficult time persuading North Atlantic swordfishermen to try a new fishing method that was discovered in 1960 and proven successful by the Japanese. Up until that time, swordfish had always been harpooned on the surface. The new method consisted of a series of baited hooks dropped into deep water and allowed to drift freely from surface buoys. Ichthyologists had determined that swordfish spend more time scouring the deeper depths than they do frolicking on the surface, but it took two years for the scientists to convince the fishermen of this. When American fishermen finally accepted the new method, their annual catches surpassed all previous records. They enjoyed this boom for nine years until scientists discovered an access of mercury in swordfish which they concluded made it dangerous to eat. The swordfish industry took a quick dip, and is only just now beginning to come back.

American scientists also persuaded the Peruvians to stop digging "guano" in 1962 and convinced them to go fishing instead. At that time, guano (bird droppings) was used for fertilizer, and processing guano was one of Peru's biggest businesses, producing a profit of $20,000,000 a year. Ichthyologists proved to the Peruvians that fish would make a better fertilizer and also could be sold as food. In other words, there was more money to be made in catching the fish that the birds ate to produce guano than there was in digging up the bird droppings. When the Peruvians finally went to sea, it was only a few months before they were catching more fish than the fishermen of any other nation in the world. Their fish meal and fish oil production alone now brings in about $150,000,000 annually.

It was Jules Verne, in his classic "Twenty Thousand Leagues Under The Sea," who predicted that, "the oceans so rich in nutrition would some day become the world's staff of life." His hero, Captain Nemo, ate only food that was harvested from the sea, and Nemo's favorite smoke was a cigar made of seaweed. Today we realize that the sea is much more fertile than the land and potentially much more productive, yet only 3% of man's food comes from the sea. The oceans are untapped storehouses of natural wealth and we've only just begun to exploit these resources. Although 88 billion pounds of fish are caught and consumed in the world every year, many edible species are not fished at all and the few desirable species are being over-fished, to the point where some are threatened with extinction.

American fishermen net 300 different types of fish, but 60% of the catch is made up of only nine species, including shrimp, tuna, cod and haddock. Over 80% of the fish consumed in the United States is imported from other countries. The people from most other countries eat more fish than Americans; for example, fish makes up about 40% of Russia's diet and close to 60% of the Japanese diet. The average American eats only about 15 pounds of seafood every year. However, with the anticipated population explosion, America will either have to catch or import some 4 billion pounds more per year by the year 2020, just to keep up with our meager demand for seafood.

In 1962, almost 50% of all fish consumed in the world were caught by Japanese fishermen. America was the second largest fish producer and Peru was third. In 1964, the tide turned and Peru led the list by netting 51.6 million metric tons of fish, Japan was second, Communist China was third, followed by Russia and the Untied States. The bulk of Peru's enormous catch is "anchovetas," a fish that is only 3 to 6 inches long. By 1970, Peru was providing four times the American catch and fishermen of Russia, Japan and Communist China were bringing in twice the American haul. Today the United States has slipped to seventh place, capturing only about 5% of the world's annual fish supply. There are many reasons why Americans are being out-fished, but the main reason is that other countries like Russia, Germany, Norway and Japan are using modern techniques and equipment while American fishermen are still struggling with outdated nets being hauled from antiquated fishing vessels. One of America's top fishing ports, Gloucester, Massachusetts, had 265 fishing vessels in 1950. Now it has less than 100 and most of them are from 20 to 60 years old. The Gloucester fishing ships are so old and unseaworthy that 14 of them were lost at sea in the 1980s and since then, an average of three per year have been lost or put into mothballs.

"It's a sad commentary on world economics," said Dr. Herbert Graham, former Director of the U.S. Bureau of Commercial Fisheries, "that foreign fishermen catch fish off our shore, frequently fishing alongside our own fleet; process the fish in their own countries and export it to the U.S. in direct competition with our own product..." and today it is an even sadder commentary, for many recent restrictions have been imposed by our government on America's commercial fishermen.

At Georges Banks, America's most productive fishing grounds located off New England, vessels from many nations, including Britain, Canada, Japan, Germany, Poland and Russia, fish side by side. In this area, where the cold Labrador Current meets the warm Gulf Stream, fish are plentiful and although close to the Massachusetts coast, the good fishing is outside America's twelve mile limit in international waters; therefore, foreign vessels are allowed to fish there.

The average size of Russian, Japanese and German fishing trawlers is about 270 feet. American trawlers average 70 to 80 feet. Russia has from 175 to 300 fishing vessels continuously working off America's East Coast. These "Supertrawlers" use the latest equipment in locating and catching fish, including ultrasonic echo sounders that can spot schools of fish in the depths. Their ships also carry electric current devices that force fish to the surface and funnels them into a trap. Then the fish are sucked up into the boat through flexible hoses by a vacuum pump. This pump can suck up 7 tons of fish in 10 minutes. Some of the Russian ships also have hydrostats, pressure resistant windowed chambers that can lower men to a depth of 1,500 feet, where they can watch and study the migration of the fish they are about to catch. The Russian and Japanese fleets also employ quick freezing ammonia refrigeration to keep fish at temperatures of 20° to 0° F. The majority of their trawlers have 3,000 ton hold capacities and are entirely stern net operated, allowing them to catch about 25 tons of fish in one sweep. Rhode Island fishermen have reported that once the Russians are on the scene off Nantucket Shoals, "our landings drop from 900 tons of fish a week to 200 tons a week." Columbus Islen of Woods Hole, known as The Father of Oceanography, once said at a meeting of scientists in Boston, that "the Russian and Japanese have the most advanced fishing methods. The Russians process their fish at sea and what they throw away the American fishermen get."

All fish processing on Russian factory ships is fully mechanized. There products include frozen fish, fillets, fish meal, canned fish and fish fat. After two months of fishing, a Russian trawler returns home with over 700 tons of fresh fish, plus canned fish and fish meal. Two of Russia's fishing boats, the AVKARIUM I and II, can transport over 30 tons of fish alive in metallic holds from American fishing grounds to their home port. The fish remain alive in water that is oxygenated by an injector device. This system allows the Russians to transport fish from our waters to theirs and someday they may develop their own superb fishing grounds like Georges Bank.

Russia has a new multipurpose factory ship of 43,000 tons, which carries 14 large fishing boats and has its own cannery aboard, capable of producing 150,000 cans of fish a day. The Russians also use submarines to scout and study fish in American waters. Their research sub, SEVERYANKA, has made seven cruises to North Atlantic waters.

One of the main reasons Russia intensified its undersea research and began developing advanced fishing techniques is because in the mid-1930s, they completely fished out the herring supply in the Caspian Sea and the Sea of Azov. The Russians moved on to more productive waters off Africa and America, where they again threaten to deplete these areas of edible fish. Off the New England coast, Russian ships line up, side by side, sometimes almost 200 of them and they sweep an area clean of all sea life. Many times they sweep through and destroy American lobster traps and fish nets, but the American fishermen have been unsuccessful in suing for damages. The Russians are not only completely outfishing us in our own backyard, but seriously threaten to fish out our most productive grounds at a time when we may be forced to turn to the sea to meet food demands.

The Japanese also have a modern, efficient fishing fleet and they have been instrumental in developing much of the automated equipment used in fishing today. Japanese fishermen use underwater electrical sound devices that herd schools of fish and direct them into a pumping mechanism which lifts the fish into the ships by the ton. The positive electrode in the water actually directs the muscle control of fish and forces them to swim toward the electrode like a pack of rodents following the Pied Piper. The Japanese use this device almost exclusively to catch herring. They also invented a detector that can spot fish swimming at depths up to 1,000 feet and literally sandwich their position for fishermen. The only drawback to this device is that it can only detect tuna fish and was aptly dubbed the "Tuna fish Sandwicher." Recently, the detector was perfected to spot schools of other species as well. Another invention by the Japanese used to catch tuna and albacore, is an artificial octopus made of vinyl. Scientists at Tokai University tested this and other methods of catching tuna with pole and line for eight years and found that the vinyl likeness of the octopus lured schools of tuna better than any other artificial means.

Tuna fishing in Australia is controlled to a great degree by airplanes carrying radiometers which detect water temperature differences. Airplanes flying at 1,200 feet over the water trailing radiometers, relay ocean temperatures back to the fishermen who are acutely aware of the range of water temperatures that tuna fish desire. Water temperature data is also provided by the U.S. Navy to guide West Coast tuna fishermen. Utilizing these water temperature sensing devices, the American Department of Interior is gathering information on the migration of sport and commercial fish. They are also pinning down ocean circulation patterns to find out how fish eggs and feed drift through various temperature zones. Thusfar they have discovered that bluefish will enter waters where the temperature is 60° but will leave the area when the temperature goes to 70°. Mackerel like temperatures between 48° and 52° and striped bass avoid water temperatures below 42°.

Sardine fishermen also use airplanes to aid them in locating fish, but their planes do not carry water temperature meters; they merely search the seas for flocks of seagulls. The sharp eyed gulls are the first to spot the metallic gleam of a sardine school and when the pilot locates the gulls he calls in the sardine fleet. More times than not however, the sardines that are netted commercially are not sardines at all. The sardines of Norway are actually a fish called "bristling" and the Portuguese sardine is a pilchard. Even the canned sardines that are caught and produced in our own state of Maine are really baby herrings.

A fairly new innovation to reveal the habits, wanderings and growth rates of certain fish, is fish "tagging." Probably the biggest fish tagging program was recently undertaken by the U.S. Department of Interior in Oregon and Washington, where 32,000,000 Chinook salmon were tagged and released. Herring are also being tracked by clamping plastic disks with information such as place and date of release to the side of their heads. When these tagged herring are caught by fishermen, the date and exact location of the catch is passed on to the agency that is conducting the experiment. Off the New England coast, $1.00 is offered for the capture of a tagged yellowtail flounder and recently one trawl fisherman brought up 50 tagged flounder in his net. Also, at Georges Bank, a blackback flounder was recently re-caught, 4 1/2 years after it was tagged and released at Block Island, some 200 miles away. The U.S. Bureau of Commercial Fisheries has had many herring and flounder tags returned as of late and some fishermen have actually mailed the fish back to the bureau, which is a practice they would like to discourage.

Trying to tag 150 lb. tuna fish is a slow and sometimes dangerous process. The tuna is first captured on a hook, then hauled aboard a research ship. It is laid on a sponge mat and blind-folded. The blind-fold actually immobilizes the tuna for half a minute, during which time a plastic tag is injected into its fin. The tuna is then released. One bluefish tuna, tagged in August, 1962 at Baja, California, was recaptured in July 1968 off the coast of Japan. It weighed 29 lbs. when it was released and 171 lbs. when captured. Another tuna weighing 22 lbs. when tagged in 1993 off California, was also caught off Japan in 1995. It weighed only 67 lbs. but had traveled 4,820 miles within the two years.

Radioactive pellets, or "sonic tags" as they are sometimes called, are being inserted into the stomachs of fish. In the herring industry, these internally tagged fish are discovered in the processing plants by means of a detecting device. Also, battery powered electronic transmitters have been employed to trace schools of fish with sonic tags. These transmitters were used to follow

Schools of fish, so thick you can hardly see the water they swim in, are sometimes encountered by scuba divers.
Photo by Ron Church.

salmon migration in the Columbia River and the movements of tagged shad in Maryland's Susquehanna River. Recent research has also shown that a transmitter can be placed surgically in a fish's stomach with a gold battery that is powered by the natural acids in its stomach.

Ichthyologists are also experimenting with the use of oral administrations of drugs to capture big and dangerous fish for tagging. The drugs are released underwater and swallowed by the fish and in turn, absorbed into its system. This renders a dangerous fish unconscious long enough for tags to be clamped to its body, or sonic tags sewn into its stomach. Hypodermic projectiles called "hypospears" are also being used by divers to capture and tag big fish. The diver shoots the hypospear into the fish and knocks it out, giving him time to administer the tagging device underwater. Fish and Game Departments have also hired scuba divers to tag fish by shooting eight inch needles with tags on them directly into the fish's tail.

Underwater lights are a popular means of attracting fish and in the Caspian Sea, bright flood lights are used to harvest fish into huge suction pumps. During one of the fish study missions of the Russian submarine SEVERYANKA, the depth at 500 feet was illuminated with flood lights and attracted thousands of herring. The fish dashed themselves against the lights like moths to a lightbulb. The Russians are experimenting with moving sources of submarine lights to entice fish into giant suction pumps. In sports fishing, a glow powder has been perfected which is sprinkled over lures and live bait. This chemical causes the bait to shine brightly in the depths and has proven to be quite successful at catching fish, but it is outlawed in many of the popular fishing spots in the United States.

The Russians are also experimenting with sound as a means of attracting fish. They have recorded the noisy chatterings of herring and then played back the tapes in the depths as a decoy to attract live herring into their nets. American scientists are now working on a new sonar device that will locate fish by sounds rather than the presently available visual chart-like sonar equipment. A specific sound on this sonar will not only pinpoint a school of fish but will tell the fisherman what specie of fish has been located. Another recently developed fishing aid is a perforated plastic hose which is fixed to the ocean bottom and produces a multitude of air bubbles. Maine herring fisherman are now using this hose to corral fish to a collecting point where nets are then used to haul the fish aboard. In Europe, various types of underwater explosives are being tested that will kill certain species of fish but not others. In the Adriatic and Aegean Seas, fishermen have for many years used explosives to catch fish, but this method is outlawed in many parts of the world.

Back in the early 1930s, haddock fishermen were netting about 125 million fish per year, but they were throwing away approximately 75 million of their catch. The throwaways were undersized haddock that could not be marketed and 90% of them were dead when they were returned to the sea. Had these baby haddock had the opportunity to grow for just one more year, they could have provided an added decade of food for the haddock lovers of the world, and a great profit for the fishermen. This waste continued until the early 1950s, when all haddock fishermen finally accepted a new type of net with larger mesh that allow undersized fish to swim through. Although the fishermen of America, Britain, Spain, France, Canada and Russia agreed to fish with these larger mesh nets, the agreement may have come too late to save the haddock fishing industry. Their previous excessive fishing has seriously depleted the haddock grounds and annual catches are continuously decreasing.

The herring fishermen are also threatening the population of that species, and Canadian fishermen are suffering their worst herring seasons in decades. Canadian and American salmon catches have also been steadily declining since 1951. In America's North West, salmon fisheries are in jeopardy because of over-fishing and the state of Washington has limited the number of fishermen licensed to catch salmon. In order to stop excessive salmon fishing at Bristol Bay, Alaska, officials deemed it unlawful to fish from motorized boats. Fishermen must have their boats towed to the fishing grounds and then sail their boats about the grounds chasing salmon. Halibut fishing is also on the decline, mainly because the returns are too small for the time, effort and initial equipment expenses. Today, almost 50% of halibut fishermen in the United States are over 60 years of age and the young men are refusing to follow their fathers into the business.

Many experts believe that over-exploitation of edible species and poor conservation methods seriously threaten the fishing industry and may upset the essential life balance of the undersea world. Pollution, of course, is a main factor contributing to fish kills. A recent report from the Federal Water Quality Control Administration stated the 40.6 million fish died in polluted waters in 45 states within one year. According to this report, industry is responsible for 70% of the fish kills, and fertilizers, detergents and insecticides killed about 25% of the fish. Synthetic detergents widely used in homes and industry, even though they may travel through waste treatment plants, do not break down and when consumed by fish, kills them. Fish are dying by the millions in rivers such as the Mississippi, and the Public Health Service believes they are victims of powerful pesticides being used against weeds and bugs. At Geisenkeim, Germany in 1971, two barrels of the insecticide "endosulfan" fell into the Rhine River killing 40 million fish at an estimated loss of $625,000 to commercial fishermen. Birds called petrels, living on the Bermuda Islands, face extinction because of DDT. This deadly chemical used as a pesticide is consumed by the fish who are eaten by the petrels and the birds have been dying off in alarming numbers.

At the turn of the century, sturgeons were caught in great numbers in the Hudson River, New York, and were sold commercially as "Albany Beef." Sturgeon also provided an annual $6,000,000 business in caviar. Within thirty years, pollution killed a thriving business and 98% of the fish.

There are many examples of pollution wiping out fish populations. Here are a few from the American files: a tank of dithane is accidentally dumped into a ditch leading to a river—4,100 fish killed; an over dosage of xylene is used as aquatic weed control—4,000 fish killed; rain washes cresote off a highway into a lake—600 fish killed; a southern railroad company spills two tanks of photo-finishing fluids into a river—5,000 fish killed; a sewage treatment plant is forced to bypass pipes and uses a local river—6,000 fish killed.

In Anderson County, Kentucky a few years ago, a seven story whiskey warehouse collapsed during a fire, hurling barrels of bourbon into a nearby river. It was, one official stated, "the biggest highball ever made." Thousands of intoxicated fish floated dead to the surface. A similar "scotch highball" was mixed at Blodneck, Scotland in 1961, when a distillery worker accidentally allowed 5000 fifths of whiskey to drain into a river. Thousands of dead fish washed up on shore, but as one local villager commented, "It made the fish exceptionally tasty."

At Gloucester, Massachusetts, New England's leading fishing port since the time of the Pilgrims, not only are government restrictions limiting where and for what fish local fishermen can utilize their nets, drags and hooks, but in the 1990's, their catch has consisted of dangerous discarded waste. Captain Sal LoGrasso, whose been fishing out of Gloucester for over thirty years, recently hauled up leaky barrels from the depth, which not only destroyed his catch, but destroyed him as well. The fumes from the barrels knocked him unconscious and gagged his crew. Toxic waste was in the barrel, and to this day the skipper suffers from constant dizzy spells, making him unable to go fishing. A similiar situation was experienced by the crew of the VITO C. out of Gloucester in 1991, when a netted drum of unknown chemicals splashed onto the deck from a net hauled from the depths. The chemical not only burned the skin off the fish, but burned the eyes and throats of the skipper and crew. "These chemical hauls are becoming increasingly common," says Bob Corbin, State Environmental Officer. Many of these leaking drums contain radioactive waste, dumped off Boston in the 1960s and 70s, close to Gloucester's lucrative fishing grounds. An estimated 4,000 barrels of radioactive waste, plus an unknown number of industrial waste barrels, deteriorating by the minute, remain off shore in New England.

One of the great problems faced by seafood consumers is eating contaminated fish that have somehow managed to survive in polluted waters. Two people in Michigan and five in Tennessee died recently from food poisoning after eating smoked whitefish. In Japan from 1970 to 1980, over 45 people died and many others suffered mental retardation and blindness from eating fish from a harbor where mercury was being deposited from a plastics factory. Swedish officials discovered that mercury contaminated fish eaten by birds were killing off the birds by the millions and today the people of Sweden are warned by their government not to eat more than one fish dinner a week.

In Canada in 1970, a university student found high concentrates of mercury in freshwater fish and immediately in parts of Canada and the United States, hundreds of lakes and rivers were closed off to commercial and sports fishermen. A few months later, 25,000 liver pills made from seals were recalled from a market by the American Food and Drug Administration because they were contaminated with mercury. The president of the West Coast company that produced the pills said that he had used seal livers for his product because "seal is supposed to be one of the most uncontaminated animals in the world—so you can figure from this that there isn't any water in the world that isn't contaminated." In December, 1970, scientists at New York State University discovered that some cans of tuna fish contained mercury in quantities well over 0.5 parts per million, the standard set by the U.S. Food and Drug Administration. The tuna industry was forced to recall over 921,000 cans of tuna fish from the American market and much of it was returned to Japan, its place of origin. Some cans were resold to Italy, France and Spain, where food standards are not as strict as in America. Charles Edwards, FDA Commissioner, said that, "The American 0.5 guidelines is extremely cautious and offers a substantial margin of safety."

After the tuna scare, all other edible species of fish were tested and it was discovered that some West Coast striped bass and some East Coast lobsters contained a high percentage of mercury, but not enough to take these delicacies off the market, although in Massachusetts, radio stations announced that pregnant women should not eat lobster. Over 90% of all swordfish tested contained mercury well over the FDA limit and, in 1971, over two million pounds of swordfish was withheld from the American market. This crippled the American and Japanese swordfish industry for years.

Mercury, which is also known as quick silver, is used by industry in the manufacture of paints, plastics, paper and various chemicals. Industrial and sometimes agricultural discharges into lakes, rivers and bays cause the mercury poisoning of fish, but scientists also believe that natural ocean deposits of mercury, consumed by small fish who are in turn consumed by big fish, may be the biggest factor.

Another pollution problem is caused by underwater algae, which is often stuffed with human waste and other organic sewage and takes away life-giving oxygen from the fish. Dr. Troy Dorris of Oklahoma State University is now testing his idea that nature may be able to take care of man-made wastes and possibly some industrial wastes as well. He has found that algae manufactures oxygen for bacteria and that the bacteria will eat the waste products. When the wastes are consumed the bacteria turns on the algae and when the algae is gone the bacteria dies, leaving clean, fresh water. Dr. Dorris is now testing his theory in a string of ponds in Oklahoma.

Another possible source of pollution and fish kills is the disposal of low-level radioactive wastes and of dangerous industrial wastes such as beryllium at designated undersea areas in the Atlantic, Pacific and Irish Sea. Studies are now underway to determine the resistance of packages in which these chemicals are contained and the possible effects of movement of these dangerous wastes due to currents and underwater storms.

Even the fish themselves have at one time or another been the source of pollution. There are many examples of 100% mortality of certain species in a given area within a twelve hour period, due to quick water temperature changes, over-crowding or infections caused by parasites. For example, the very tasty tilefish that were once caught commercially by North East fishermen, were wiped out in two days during the summer of 1882. Hundreds of millions of dead tilefish, covering 5,000 square miles from Maine to Florida, dotted the surface waters. No one knows for sure what killed them while allowing all other species to live. Some thought that a sudden change in water temperature or an underwater earthquake caused the mass killing, but then, why weren't the cod, herring, haddock, and whiting wiped out as well? One estimate at the time was that the dead tilefish could have provided 200 lbs. of fish for every person living in America.

Infections and parasites have also caused destruction to large quantities of edible fish. The amberjack for one, is often molested by a roundworm that imbeds itself in the tail section of the fish. Although amberjacks are often enthusiastically eaten by man, roundworms and all, they have caused some cases of ciguatera poisoning and for this reason some people will not eat amberjacks. Columnaris, often called "cotton-wool disease," is a bacteria that infects the mouth, skin and gills of freshwater fish. It particularly attacks salmon and trout. Recently, salmon in the rivers of England and Ireland were infected with this disease to almost epidemic proportions. The lamprey, a parasitic eel-like fish is responsible for killing millions of fish in lakes and rivers. In the 1930's through 1950's, lampreys invaded the Great Lakes and virtually wiped out the trout, especially in Lake Superior. In 1961, a chemical was introduced to the water that kills young lampreys but does not harm other fish. Since that time, trout fishing has increased dramatically in the Great Lakes.

Besides over-fishing, pollution and fish diseases, fishermen have lately been cursed with another problem. Other nations with rich and extensive fishing grounds off their coasts have closed off the grounds to outsiders. The 1960 Geneva Conference failed to resolve territorial sea boundaries mainly because all the nations could not agree on the same boundary limits. Conflict and confusion over fishing rights within claimed territorial waters is creating a sea battle that probably will not be solved for some time. The most disputed area is the most abundant fishing grounds off South America, where nine Latin American nations have set 200-mile limits. Thusfar, Ecuador has captured over 100 American tuna fishing boats and has collected over $485,000 from the American government for the safe return of these boats. An interesting sidelight to the tuna war which began in 1952, is that the Ecuadorian ships used to capture the American fishing boats were given to that country some years ago by the American government. Also, in the summer of 1971, seven American shrimp boats were forced at gun point to retreat beyond Brazil's 200-mile limit. One shrimpboat captain reported that he was fired upon by the Brazilian ships and another American fisherman said that, "They not only got after us with a gunboat, but also had aircraft overhead and a submarine beneath our ships."

Most fishermen are, by nature, optimistic always hoping for and counting on "a bigger catch tomorrow." New England fisherman also have a saying that "One door never closes but a new one opens" and a new innovation to help solve the plight of the fisherman and the increasing need for more fish is fish farming, commonly called "aquaculture." Aquaculture is the breeding of fish under controlled conditions for food purposes. Japan has advanced in this area more than any other nation and presently fish farming accounts for 7% of all fish consumed in that country. Many Japanese fishermen have been forced into taking up fish farming because of heavy pollution in their coastal waters. There are now some 1,500 such farms throughout Japan, producing 440,000 tons of fish a year, worth approximately $278,000,000.

Hamachi fish, a member of the mackerel family, are bred in large ponds surrounded by nets and are ideal for aquaculture purposes because they grow so rapidly. Hamachi fish is less than an inch long when it is born but within a year it grows to 16 inches and within two years it is 25 inches long. The Japanese farms produce 40,000 tons of hamachi each year. Other fish that are bred in Japanese farms are prawn, trout, salmon, mullet, eels and carp. At the carp farms, these fish thrive on human waste which is purposely dumped into the farm area from nearby cities.

Outside of Japanese fish farming, probably the most impressively productive forms of aquaculture take place in Italy, France, Spain, Holland and now Scotland, where recently over five acres were set aside for farming whitefish. In Europe, it is mostly oysters, clams and mussels that are grown and harvested under controlled conditions.

Always a favorite of Europeans is carp fish and it was so desired by the early American settlers that in the year 1700, five carp were shipped to America for breeding purposes. Deposited in a river, these five carp multiplied rapidly and today, carp ranks as the number two fish most taken by freshwater fishermen in this country. Carp multiply faster than rabbits and a large female may carry as many as 2,000,000 eggs. Carp can now be found in most lakes and ponds in America and in many places it has become a pest fish. They eat bass eggs and stir up the waters so badly that the bass die from lack of oxygen.

Striped bass also began a migration West in 1879, thanks to a man named Livingston Stone. He transported 162 bass by rail from New Jersey to San Francisco. When the fish arrived in San Francisco they were deposited into the bay. Up until that time there were no striped bass off the West Coast. Twenty years later, 1,234,320 lbs. of stripers were caught by fishermen in Frisco Bay and in 1992, California fishermen caught 42,000 striped bass. In 1962, 300 stripers were transported from California to Florida to supply our southern waters.

In Nevada in 1873, George and Henry Schmidtlein with two Indians, netted a quantity of native trout from the Truckee and Walker Rivers and placed them in wooden vinegar and syrup barrels filled with fresh water. They then secured the barrels to horses and traveled four days to Kingston Creek into which they dumped the fish. Only 39 trout in the vinegar kegs lived through the journey and all the fish in the syrup barrels died. The trout prospered in Kingston Creek and their offspring were then replanted into many other lakes, ponds, rivers and creeks of Nevada, where the trout fishing today is superb.

Half a century ago, British biologist Walter Garstang transplanted European flounder from the shallows of the Dutch coast to the middle of the North Sea. The flounders, once transferred, grew to three times their original size. The Chinook salmon has also been successfully transplanted from North American waters to New Zealand. The Chinook, which is in constant demand as food, spends part of its life in freshwater and part in the sea and therefore it has been the object of many experiments. Mr. Milo Moore, former Washington Director of Fisheries, championed American salmon farming and began a pilot program in Puget Sound to rear salmon in salt water rather than fresh water. In protected ponds, the young salmon are allowed to find different salinity levels of their choice before going to sea. They were hatched and released within 140 days and thusfar the salt water salmon have outgrown their freshwater cousins by over three inches. Special breeding in Puget Sound has also produced Chinook salmon that are more resistant to high water temperatures and more immune to diseases than their naturally hatched counterparts. The selected stock also matured earlier and were stronger. It is interesting to note that specially bred Chinook, when released from the Puget Sound Hatchery, travel thousands of miles and when they return three or four years later, they swim up a ladder and deposit themselves into the very same hatchery pens from which they originally came. The Pilot Salmon Research Farm Project is also developing and raising pen salmon. These salmon, when bred in captivity, will be ready for market 14 months after hatching. Presently there are 700,000 pen salmon at the Puget

Sound farm, which will soon be transferred from freshwater ponds to saltwater pens.

The selective breeding of fish to develop desired traits and characteristics was started in Japan in 1500 A.D., when the man-made goldfish "Demekin" was born after years of careful breeding. The Demekin is actually a mutation, with bulging eyes and a filament-like tail. Recently, a fish hatchery in Missouri managed to cross a goldfish with carp, but the offspring of this strange combination were sterile. In Israel, the selective breeding of carp has been most successful. At Galilee, carp grow to great size, sometimes twice the size of American carp. The Israelis are also experimenting with giving carp hormone injections and at Galilee's 300 acre reservoir, 250,000 larvae produced 120 tons of edible fish within a year. Other nations such as Haiti, have received assistance from Israel on the techniques of carp farming.

Pituitary hormones from carp were used in catfish experiments in Oklahoma, which induced successful spawning. Human hormones were also used on catfish which increased cat fry production from 82,000 to 700,000. Utilizing this artificial propagation has in most cases produced faster growing, bigger and more disease resistant fish in greater quantities. This is especially true in the selective breeding of trout. In Massachusetts and New Jersey, trout hatcheries fed the fish paprika pellets which not only increased fish egg production but increased the fish rate of growth. By using these pellets the fish became huskier, healthier and were brilliantly colored. Within four generations of selectively bred trout, the offspring measured 14 inches at maturity, four inches larger than the average length of native trout.

In addition to artificially breeding fish in special ponds and hatcheries, artificial reefs have been constructed in some offshore areas to attract fish for study purposes and to provide new grounds for sport and commercial fishermen. Artificial reefs in the Gulf of Mexico and East and West Coasts of America have been built out of every imaginable material: junk autos, street cars, old boats, rock piles, and concrete. Usually, no matter what these reefs are made of, they make excellent hiding places for the fish, added profit for the fishermen and sometimes a few extra dollars for the local junk dealer. At Montgomery Reef, Jacksonville, Florida, scuba divers built a new reef out of automobile tires, 8 1/2 miles off the coast. The hundreds of weighted auto tires were dumped in 1960 and since then fishing has improved considerably in the area. The U.S. Navy however, squelched plans for an artificial reef to be built off Miami, Florida, because it was going to be built at a depth of 100 feet, two miles off the shore and would make an excellent hiding place for any unfriendly submarines. Even the best sonar devices would not be able to distinguish a submarine from a junk car. Trolley cars were deposited in the Pacific at San Francisco to attract fish and at Santa Barbara, 120 old wrecked automobiles were used to create an underwater reef. Also off California, when a large undersea area was destroyed by oil pollution, a group of teenagers cut out strips of canvas, painted them green, attached them to cement blocks and planted them in the ocean. This was done to see if fish would be attracted to their artificial garden as they had been to the seaweed that once grew in the area. The fish came in droves and the teenagers were instrumental in bringing back fishing to an area that had been devastated by oil.

For thousands of years the sea has been ignored by scientists as a source for medicines and drugs, but recent experiments and discoveries reveal that the sea may become a most precious medicine cabinet. Seaweed is presently used in over 300 pharmaceuticals to suspend drugs and antibiotics such as penicillin. Carraghen, the seaweed element used to stabilize foods, is also used to treat patients who suffer with peptic ulcers. Dr. Leonard Worthen of the University of Rhode Island has found that Irish Moss, found along the New England and European coasts, restricts bacteria growth and another type of seaweed appears to overcome influenza viruses. Scientists in Japan, England, France and the United States are studying seaweed as a possible means to detect antibiotic activity in humans. An undersea weed found off the coast of Mexico, called "ulvalinya," is a cure for internal infections and a variety of seaweed found in the South Sea Islands has for generations been used as a remedy for skin diseases and stomach disorders.

Recent studies of fish have also produced some remarkable wonder drugs and there are other medicines from the sea that are not on the market yet and won't be until experiments are conclusive. For example, the saliva from the mouth of the octopus controls blood coagulation in humans and can be found in an agent called "eledoisin." Eledoisin is 10,000 times more powerful than any other known drug in controlling high blood pressure and irregular heartbeats. It has also been discovered that poison from the mouth of the sea-snake will coagulate blood and there is a form of algae which also hastens coagulation. Whales, seals and porpoises are now being studied in hopes that they may hold the secret cure for human heart disease. These mammals have the ability to slow down their hearts before submerging into deep water. Further study and experiments with the circulatory and respiratory systems of these creatures should provide us with invaluable information. A chemical called "holothurin," found in the West Indies sea-cucumber and in some sea urchins is a heart stimulant and may also be used in the future as a coronary treatment.

Even the lowly clam, mussel and oyster contain potent chemicals. Mussels that have eaten toxic microscopic organisms can provide an anesthetic 100,000 times more powerful than cocaine, and clams and oysters contain an antivirus called "prolin I," which arrests wound infections, strep throat, bronchial pneumonia, scarlet fever and tonsillitis. A related substance, "prolin II," when injected into mice, protected them from polio. A poison secreted by the sea snail "Conus Geopraphs," when given to humans in limited doses, relaxes muscles and is being developed as a drug to combat convulsions. A cousin to the sea snail, "Conus Magnus," provides a toxin that contracts human muscles and may be used some day to restore diseased or malfunctioning limbs.

Over half of 120 species of sponges contain antibiotics, reports the New York Aquarium's Laboratory of Marine Sciences. The red-beard sponge contains "ectyonin," which kills infectious viruses including the deadly "stophylococcus" bacteria which even penicillin is powerless against. It is now being tested as a possible combatant to bladder infections and tuberculosis. Chemicals from the blue sponge were effective in attacking gastric bacteria and may be used in the future to fight a gastric disease that has caused the death of many children. Other ingredients from a variety of sponges may someday be the cures for blood poisoning, pneumonia and arthritis. Thusfar the most important medial ingredient found in a sponge was brought to light by Dr. Seymour Cohen of the University of Pennsylvania. Dr. Cohen found that an extract from a Caribbean sponge is effective against leukemia. This sponge drug produced partial and, in some cases, complete control of leukemia in 50% of the patients he tested. This same extract may soon be used by surgeons to suppress white cells during transplant operations and to help control the spread of rabies.

There were many ancient sea remedies for various ills and diseases that scientists are looking into today, but some of them were quite unorthodox and probably did nothing for the patients. For instance, sea horses were once swallowed alive as a cure for stomach sickness in China, and pearls from oysters were boiled and consumed by warriors before they went into battle to give them courage.

Many Americans recall holding their noses as a spoonful of cod-liver oil was forced down their throats as a defense against the common cold, and in clipper ship days, sailors rubbed sunfish oil on their bumps and bruises for quick healing. Today, liver oil from many types of fish and sea mammals are used in vitamins and medicines. Even calcium phosphate from ground up fish bones is used in some medicines. In Japan, a powder derived from the liver of the puffer-fish is sold as a nerve deadener and a chemical from the rare trigger fish is used to help combat diabetes. The poisonous venom from Portuguese man-o-war provides remedies for ulcers and heart disease and Dr. Charles Richet received the Nobel Prize for discovering "anaphylaxis," a cure for allergies such as asthma, which is made from man-o-war venom. Even the tiny barnacle may soon be in demand, for the adhesive substance it excretes may soon be used as a tooth cement by dentists.

The National Cancer Institute has been experimenting with many marine animals in hopes of finding an anti-tumor substance. Thusfar, they have discovered that clams contain an ingredient that delays and in some cases prevents the development of cancer in experimental mice. Another possible anti-cancer agent is "holothurin," found in starfish and sea urchins. This agent, when injected into cancer ridden mice every other day for 20 days, sustained their lives for an additional 18 months to two years over non-injected mice. Another possible anti-cancer drug comes from the seaworm "Bonellia." This worm secretes a hormone that can determine the sex of its offspring. The baby worms in larvae stage that touch their mother stop growing and develop into males. Those that do not touch their mother grow much larger (12 inches) and become females. In experiments, scientists have discovered that the growth stopping hormone in the mother worm can also stop the growth of throat cancer cells in humans.

Off the coast of Hawaii, Dr. Francis Tabrah of the University of Hawaii, is scuba diving for little white seaworms called "Kaunaoa." The diving doctor recently discovered in old island records that Hawaiian witch doctors once boiled the tentacles of these sea worms and fed the broth to elderly natives as cure for what appeared to be cancer. After Dr. Tabrah found and captured some of these white worms, he concocted an extract from the tentacles and experimented with cancer ridden mice. His first tests showed that the worm tentacles suppressed cancer. "Now," says Dr. Tabrah, "we must separate the many chemical compounds in the tentacles and isolate the one that seems to suppress cancer." It is interesting to note that Hawaiian swimmers and fishermen have always feared the white sea worm Kaunaoa, believing that when stung by one, it could create a wound that would never heal. If either the worm Kaunaoa or Bonellia prove to contain the cure for cancer, the sea worm, without doubt, will become the greatest treasure in the sea.

Sea worms are actually fished for and eaten in some parts of the world. A worm called "Sipunculid" is a delicacy in the Orient and the sea worm "Palolo" is netted and eaten by the natives of the South Pacific. Living in the only three lakes of the Sahara Desert is the one-eighth of an inch long saltwater worm called a "dood." The men who fish for these little creatures are called "Dauadas," which in Arabic means "worm men." After being netted, doods are pounded into a black paste, rolled into a ball and dried to sell at the market for food. The very subsistence of these Northern Sahara natives is dependent on the food provided by these worms.

In the nearby Sudan and Eritrea, bordering the Red Sea, natives spear stingrays for food, but will not eat the sweet clams that are abundant in the shallows. The Eritreans eat sea urchins and the people of Central America and the Caribbean Islands eat the ripe gonards of sea urchins when the urchin is breeding in the Spring. The gonards are sometimes cooked, but often eaten raw. There are 200 fishing vessels that leave Madagascar each week in search of sea-cucumbers. This marine animal, netted in tropical waters, resembles the land cucumber in shape and size and although somewhat toxic, is a favored food in the Far East. In the Fiji Islands, sea-cucumbers are cut up and boiled to make a tasty soup. On the atolls of Oceania, natives survive on urchins and fish but will eat lobsters only in times of famine. In France, Greece and Italy, a food that is growing in popularity is the sea anemone, which is said to taste much like lobster. Since ancient times in France and Italy, mullet has been considered a delicacy and it has always been cooked and eaten with its intestines intact. A century ago it was discovered that twelve inch tapeworms live in the intestines of most mullets, but apparently this didn't bother too many Frenchmen or Italians, for the mullet is still devoured in those countries, entrails, tapeworms and all. Also a favorite food in Europe is eel, but polluted waters have depleted their supply, so over 100 tons of long-finned eels from New Zealand and Australia are imported every year. The wolf-fish, an ugly eel-like creature of the North Atlantic is thrown away when netted by American fishermen, yet in Iceland the wolf-fish is considered an extremely delicious food. Also, those who have eaten toadfish consider it to be one of the best tasting fish in the Atlantic, but the toadfish is so ugly looking that very few people will buy it at the fish market. North Atlantic fishermen say that the toadfish is one of the easiest fish to catch and at times it seems that they want to be caught. In the West Indies, natives eat sand fleas. The sand flea is no bigger than a pinhead and is often seen hopping about sandy beaches and although it may not appear appetizing, it is related to the shrimp. A chowder or soup made of sand fleas is said to taste superb.

The staff of life of all oceans and seas is plankton, tiny and almost transparent animal and vegetable particles that is the food for many fish and marine mammals. Plankton is also eaten regularly by the natives of Thailand, where fishermen capture these minute particles in fine meshed nets. Although bitter tasting, mixed with meat or fish it is said to have a delicious flavor and it contains 60% protein, plus minerals and carbohydrates. A few marine scientists have predicted that someday all humans will be forced to eat plankton for lack of other available foods.

A new product called Seachips, made from crabs, clams and oysters, is now on the American market as a snackfood. Originator of the Seachip is H. Paul Walter of General Chip Corporation, Maryland. Mr. Walter got the idea for Seachips while in Hong Kong. There he saw Chinese fishermen sun-drying a paste made from shrimp. The dried material was cooked and sold commercially and did not deteriorate for many days. Fishermen of New Bedford, Massachusetts, are experimenting with making fish and scallop chips that may last for months without spoiling. Someday, dried trash fish and plankton may be part of our daily diet. It is interesting to note that these dried, high protein fish foods not only stay fresh for a long time, but they don't smell fishy.

In Burlington, Massachusetts, a company called Singco, Inc., has come up with an ozone treatment that takes away the smell of fish. "This ozone," says a company spokesman, "kills odor-creating bacteria and de-smells fishing boats, fish warehouses, fish processing plants, and will even rid the notorious stigma from fishermen." Another, seemingly more important contribution to the fishing industry, is an antibiotic drug which combats cold-loving bacteria in fish. Fish deteriorate quickly even in iced storage because of this bacteria. Adding this drug, called "terramycin" to the ice, kills the bacteria and helps preserve the fish.

Although humans don't like the strong scent of fish, Mr. S.E. Gibbs of Corydon, Iowa, says that fish don't like the smell of humans either. Mr. Gibbs created a company called Fish Scent Laboratories, where scented chemicals and bait are distributed to fishing lure dealers throughout the world. Mr. Gibbs, convinced that fish have an exceptional sense of smell, reports that his business is quite successful. To add weight to Mr. Gibbs' theory, the Canadian Fisheries Research Board in 1951, announced to all salmon fishermen that they might enhance their catch if they wore gloves when handling bait instead of bare hands—the reason being that some secretion from human hands might be offensive to fish. It therefore may be valid to suggest to all fishermen that possibly the most important item to take on a fishing trip is a bar of soap.

In 1955, an Illinois chemist names Ezra Levin came up with a new product that could cheaply feed the starving millions of the world. He developed a process for making fish protein concentrate, also known as FPC, or fish flour. FPC is an odorless, tasteless powder made from whole fish, including head, tail and intestines. It contains 80-90% protein, whereas eggs have only 11% protein, beef 11%, and milk 35%. Presently, 500 million humans suffer from malnutrition because of lack of protein, a more frequent cause of death than any disease. By using the whole fish to make FPC, handling and cleaning costs are eliminated and any fish, including trash fish can be used to make the flour. The result is that FPC sells for 15¢ a pound, making it the cheapest, most nutritious food product available in the world.

FPC is so concentrated that one tablespoon-full a day, mixed with any other food, would give a man or child the needed day's supply of protein, which means that for $1.50, a person could buy enough for one year. FPC is produced by Mr. Levin's company called VioBin Corporation of Monticello, Illinois. He also has a plant in New Bedford, Massachusetts, turning out 15 tons of fish flour a day. At the New Bedford plant, fish are pumped from the boats into a grinding machine, then oil and water is removed from the fish and a secret process separates out bone particles. FPC is of great benefit to fishermen who have long been plagued with having to dispose of unmarketable trash fish they so often catch. Usually these unwanted fish are shoveled over the side of the boat, but now they can sell trash fish for FPC. Presently, trash fish represent about 50% of the world's total fish catch, which means fishermen could conceivably double their annual profits by using trash fish to make fish flour. Mexican fishermen actually have portable fish meal plants aboard their ships and in the future, many fishermen may be able to produce fish flour the minute they haul their nets. "FPC," says Ezra Levin, "is the doorway to peace...A man may hate you, but you feed his hungry child and he'll love you forever."

The biggest set back to FPC was, and to some degree still is, America's Food and Drug Administration. They refused to approve domestic use of fish flour on the grounds that it was "filthy" and unfit for use by Americans because it was made from whole fish. Because of this action, other countries felt that if fish flour wasn't good enough for America, it wasn't good enough for them. However, Peru, Indonesia, Pakistan, Chile, Mexico, Nigeria, Ceylon, Brazil, Bolivia, San Salvador and Thailand, did use fish flour in limited quantities to feed their hungry. Ezra Levin was, to say the least, upset that the FDA wouldn't accept FPC and he called one of the FDA members to his face, "the damnedest fool I ever met." Levin sold the fish flour as animal feed until 1967, when pressure from the U.S. Congress and President Johnson forced the Food and Drug Administration to change its mind. They approved FPC, not as a regular food, but as a food additive. Today, fish flour is shipped from America to the starving peoples of some thirty countries. One African community refused FPC however, and the local leader explained that his people "will not eat food we cannot smell or taste."

"Within 15 years," stated Dr. Frederico Gomez, leading scientist of Mexico, "fish flour could change the entire economic and social face of the world."

According to a recent study by the Food and Agricultural Organization of the United Nations, the world's need for fish is expected to reach over 100 million tons per year by the year 2000. Presently, well over 50% of the world's population is under-nourished or starving and the population is rising much faster than food production. A special United States Presidential Advisory Committee, studying the world food crisis, recently concluded that, "The world faces a food crisis of staggering proportions unless affluent nations immediately undertake a massive, long-range, innovative effort unprecedented in human history."

There is an old Chinese proverb that, "If you give a man a fish, you feed him for one day; if you teach a man to fish, you feed him for many, many days." Therefore, the best solution to the world's hunger problem may not be fish flour or surplus foods from affluent nations, but the feeding of fishing knowledge and techniques to the suffering nations. Japan, for example, has twice as many people per square mile as India has, yet the Indians are starving and the Japanese are prosperous, mainly because the Japanese rely on fishing and sea products for survival. Americans, through the Peace Corps, have taught the natives of the Congo new fishing methods and have provided outboard motors for African canoes to give them easy access to the open sea and untapped fishing grounds. In Afghanistan, Americans provided fishermen with new strong nylon nets to replace their outdated, ineffective nets and much more is being done in under-developed countries to show them that their future is in the sea.

It does seem somewhat erroneous that Americans are abroad teaching others the value of fishing when our own fishing fleet is in such disrepair, but American scientists have come up with some intriguing ideas for bettering our harvest from the sea. In the experimental stages are automatic buoys that will be placed off our coasts to detect fish and relay this information to fishermen. Also, artificial floating rafts will drift with the currents and attract fish. Aboard will be detecting apparatus and fishing boats will be signaled automatically when schools of fish accumulate near the raft. The American tuna industry has already tested these rafts off Hawaii. In the near future, huge sonar nets will be used to fence in schools of fish and it's possible that submarines may someday herd fish with electrical shocks. Also, helicopters could round up fish by dropping various chemicals in the sea. Some scientists believe that porpoises and killer whales can be trained to herd fish like dogs herd sheep and as one scientist commented, "A land farmer can fence in his stock and there is no reason why a fisherman has to deal with a wondering stock." It is proposed by two chemical engineers, Dr. J. Marchello and P.A. Martino to the University of Maryland staff, that waste heat can be used to farm the sea. Their idea is to plow the ocean bottom by using a nuclear furnace to heat deep water and make it rise upward, providing nutrient rich water to the sunlight and more plankton for feeding fish. It has also been suggested that we could improve the sea floor production by dragging comb-like devices over the bottom, as we now plow the land. Union Carbide Company has even suggested growing vegetables, such as radishes, lettus and cabbages on the ocean floor by pumping air through the salt water. One interesting thought about such farms in the sea is that they would require no fertilizer, no tillage and no rain. Although such ideas may seem farfetched, man now must seriously turn to the sea for his food and if he does not, the consequence could be worldwide famine.

American fishermen drop their nets and pray for a good catch, but foreign fishermen in bigger an more efficient ships are out fishing us in our own backyard - depleated fish supplies, pollution and strict government regulations, are slowly but surely destroying the American fishing industry.

V
DEEP DARK SEA

The crewman assigned to the midnight watch aboard the balsawood raft TAHITI-NUI, "went stark-raving mad," reported the craft's skipper Eric DeBisschop. He and a crew of four were sailing in the sturdy raft from Tahiti to the coast of South America, and were some 70 miles off Chile on January 3, 1957, when the unbelievable incident took place. "I didn't see the creature," said DeBisschop, a renowned explorer, "but the crewman, who wishes to remain anonymous, is a most reliable man, and it took hours to bring him back to his senses."

As the crewman stood his watch, he saw a seven-foot sea creature, which he described as half-human and half-fish, with seaweed-like hair, climb aboard the TAHITI-NUI just before dawn. It stood upright on its long tail and approached the astonished crewman. It scowled at him, he later reported, then slapped him across the face with such force that he hit the deck. Then, the ugly smelly creature jumped back into the sea. Captain DeBisschop realized that the crewman might have been hallucinating, but even when they touched shore a few days later, the crewman was still noticeably shaken, and, adds DeBisschop, "his face, where the creature had struck him, was covered with red welts and pieces of florescent fish scales...Possibly it was one of those unknown creatures that lives in the bowels of the ocean and comes up to the surface to feed at night."

Dave Taylor and John Boggs of Kodiak, were fishing in Zamovia Strait, Alaska, on August 6, 1979, when they spotted a weird three-foot blue fish, swimming in circles on the surface waters. "Its phosphorescent scales were fringed with purple and gold," reported Taylor, "and it had nostrils like a human, and a thick human-like tongue, but no teeth." The men managed to haul it into their boat, flapping wildly, but when they touched it they were knocked across the deck by what felt like an electric shock. They packed the strange fish in ice to preserve it for marine biologists to look at when they returned to shore. The biologists were baffled too, and many came to study it. It was beautiful but ugly, looked like a bass, but was not one. Although it had what looked like nostrils, it also had what looked like four sets of gills. The biologists decided it was of some unknown species, living in the deep, dark sea.

Imagine the fright of Ruth Kuhn and Donna Rowell, while strolling Jensen Beach at Stuart, Florida, on the morning of August 12, 1964, when they came upon a fifteen-foot monster wallowing in the shallows. It had a red mane like a rooster, and looked like an eel with tentacles sticking out of its head. Lucky for the girls the creature was dead. They immediately contacted the Institute of Marine Science at the University of Miami, and marine biologists rushed to Jensen Beach with ice-packs, not for the faint-hearted girls, but the red-headed fish, to preserve it. The biologists were soon able to identify the monster as a member of the crestfish family, a rare specimen hardly ever seen in shallow water. It was a "roosterfish" that lives thousands of feet beneath the waves.

Off the Queen Charlotte Islands, Canada, in 1934, a fisherman pulled up a creature on his hook that was only six inches long, but its mouth was bigger than its body, had big eyes, and its skin was luminescent. No one had ever seen a fish like this, but another was fished up off Port Hardy, Canada in 1972, this time by a member of the Canadian Fisheries Research Department. The fish was preserved for study. In the laboratory, Canadian biologists determined that although the fish had large eyes, it was almost totally blind. A retractable rod carried on its forehead with a light on the tip of it, they decided, was used to lure smaller fish into its huge mouth. They were also able to identify the fish as a member of the "onierodidae" family, "one of the deep sea Mafia families," joked one biologist, "that lives at 14,000 feet and can swallow fish twice its size."

Some deep water creatures do come to the surface at night looking for food. They often follow deep scattering layers of plankton, made up of minute particles of animals and plants, that rise from the deep at night when the upper waters cool. Lantern fish, living at 1,000 to 3,000-foot depths, have been seen in schools on the surface in the Antarctic. The skipper of the British steamer WEATHER OBSERVER, cruising off Glasgow, Scotland, in May, 1982, reported cruising for five hours through a sparkling display of lantern fish, that had apparently come to the surface of feed on krill. The lantern fish is only four to six-inches long and looks much like any other fish, but it has flashing light organs growing on its head and body that sparkle in a multitude of bright colors. When a new day dawns, the lantern fish return to their nightmarish world of bitter cold and perpetual darkness.

Marine scientists call this virtually unexplored world "the abyss," and only within the last fifty years has anyone even attempted to visit it. It is the last and largest of the earth's frontiers, and yet its mysteries have been with us since Adam and Eve. The abyss, from 800-foot depths to 35,800-foot depths, is where no sunlight ever penetrates, and its 115,000,000 square miles make up 61% of the earth's surface, with an average depth of 18,000-feet. Here on land we experience a constant pressure of 14.7 pounds of pressure per square inch on our bodies, whereas in the abyss, every creature experiences a constant seven to eight tons of pressure per square inch on its body. Besides eternal night and crushing pressures, the intense cold can immediately sap man's energy, and if the cold won't do it, the bone chilling fright of real or imaginary monsters lurking in the darkness surely will. It is the uncharted, untamed, and untouched part of our world, and now that man has decided to probe it, in each visit, he inevitably makes a new discovery. With each discovery, it seems, a new mystery originates. Yet, 120 years ago, most scientists were convinced that, "where sunlight does not penetrate, no life can exist."

"The popular notion was," wrote British marine scientist Sir Wyville Thomson in 1872, "that after arriving at a certain depth the conditions become so peculiar, as to preclude any other idea than that of a wasteland of utter darkness, subjected to such stupendous pressures, as to make life of any kind impossible." Another leading naturalist, Edward Forbes, had written thirty years earlier that, "the concentration of life in the sea decreases as the depth increases." He concluded, "that beyond 1,800 feet, there is no life at all in the oceans." Forbes reported to his fellow scientists that the various odd looking worms and starfish previously hauled to the surface on sounding lines from deep water, did not live in the abyss, but had attached their little bodies to the lines as the lines were being pulled through shallower water. Forbes' conclusions took "the deep-six," however, on May 10, 1876. That was the day Wyville Thomson and a few of his inquisitive friends returned to England aboard the H.M.S. CHALLENGER, after a three-and-one-half year oceanographic research voyage around the world. They had gathered marine specimens from depths of up to three miles, and had brought back over 4,700 new species of sea animals that no one had ever seen or heard of before. The CHALLENGER voyage still holds the record as the longest and most successful ocean science expedition in history.

Using a newly invented net-dredge, Thomson and his associates dragged the muddy bottoms of every ocean in the world. "It was a thrill beyond my dreams," he said, "bringing up specimens from the deep, but the greatest thrill was to bring up something alive and moving from such crushing depths. It was the biggest surprise," said Thomson. "As it rolled out of our dredge and settled quietly on deck...It was the form of a round cake, and it began to pant like a dog...I had to summon up some resolution before taking the weird little monster in my hand." It was a new type of sea urchin, taken from waters over three times the depth where Forbes said there would be no life.

The CHALLENGER scientists were also first to record the constant near-freezing temperatures in the abyss, and they took many soundings in an attempt to determine just how deep the oceans are. For each deep water sounding, it took the crew 2 1/2 hours just to let out the weighted line and to reel it in again. The deepest spot they found was in the Pacific Ocean, off Guam in the Marianas Trench, with a sounding of 26,850 feet. A deeper sounding in the same area was made 100 years later from the Russian research vessel VITIAZ, of 36,173 feet.

The first person to venture into the abyss was American zoologist William Bebee, in 1930. Bebee and Otis Barton invented and built a bathysphere, a spherical steel ball with portholes and external search lights for observation in the deep sea. Suspended by cable to a surface ship, the bathysphere was

A light emitting seven-foot squid was hauled up from the abyss at the Gulf of Maine in 1991. Photos courtesy Smithsonian Institute, Washington, D.C.

dropped to a depth of 1,300 feet. On another dive to 3,000 feet in 1932, Bebee and Barton reported seeing many strange new creatures, including one that looked somewhat like a barracuda, but had teeth that glowed, and a body that radiated a bluish light. "It was over six feet in length," said the excited Bebee upon his return to the surface, "and since I was the first to see it, I think I have the right to name it." He called it, "The Untouchable." He also reported seeing, "a school of brilliantly illuminated lantern fish with pale green lights swim past within three feet of my window. Their lights were exceedingly bright and seemed to glow steadily, and they sometimes had a pale yellow tint." Bebee and Barton also saw, "hundreds of shrimp whose bodies flashed like red flashbulbs...and a twenty-foot creature that did not have eyes or fins, but swam with little effort...and a strange looking shark with pop-eyes."

To improve on Bebee's bathysphere, two Swiss scientists, famous balloonists Auguste Piccard and his son Jacques, invented the bathyscaph. Its advantages were that it didn't need a cable or line to the surface ship, it could be navigated up to a mile in any direction underwater, and it could move up and down at the will and whim of the two pilots inside, hovering at any depth they desired. It was a round steel ball like Bebee's bathysphere, linked to a gasoline filled float-like balloon. To sink the bathyscaph, water was allowed into the float, and to ascend, some of the ten tons of iron pellets used as ballast were released. As the vessel lifted, the gas expanded, pushing out the water in the float. The Piccards built their first bathyscaph in Belgium in 1947, but it was damaged a year later in sea trials off Cape Verde Island. It was rebuilt and acquired by the French Navy, who broke all deep diving records with it on February 15, 1954, penetrating the abyss to 13,000 feet, off the coast of Dakar, Senegal. On a subsequent dive to 6,900 feet off Sicily, with four French scientists aboard, spotlights and mackerel baited hooks were attached to the outer hull of the bathyscaph to attract fish. The wide-eyed scientists peered through the portholes as large slant-eyed sharks, in a feeding frenzy, ripped at the bait, swallowing the hooks and then spitting them out like seeds. They reported seeing a large ray-like fish with bulging eyes and an antenna-like dorsal fin, a foot-long black sea-spider, a plant that walked along the bottom, and a fish with two tails that looked like legs, which it used to hop along the mud bottom like a cricket. The scientists were awe-struck, and were quick to inform their colleagues that the abyss was not only teeming with life, but made up of unique life forms never before imagined by man.

Prior to this excursion into the abyss by French scientists, who spent hours in the bathyscaph studying newly discovered marine animals, most deep sea exploration had been conducted from surface vessels with dredge-nets and various sampling and recording devices dropped into the sea on long cables. Although effective scientific study of the abyss is still conducted from the surface by oceanographic research vessels, the Piccard bathyscaph was instrumental in launching the scientific study of these strange new creatures in their own environment. It was Jacques Piccard again, who designed and built the bathyscaph TRIESTE for the United States Navy, and on January 23, 1960, the TRIESTE made the entire world sit up and take notice of the abyss. On that day, Piccard and the U.S. Navy Lieutenant Donald Walsh plunged to the deepest spot on the ocean floor, to 35,800 feet at Marianas Trench in the Pacific.

"There was light outside the TRIESTE until 800 feet," reported Walsh, "and at 6,000 feet, the chill from the water forced us to don warmer clothes." The entire descent took four hours and 48 minutes, and when they reached bottom at the very deepest spot in the underwater world, they remained there for twenty minutes, recording data and peering out the portholes. What they saw defied belief—living at 35,800 feet, under 600 atmospheres of pressure, was a foot-long flounder and a tiny shrimp. This dispelled any further argument over the inability of life to exist in the bowels of the sea. There is life everywhere in the sea. What bothered marine biologists now, however, was why did the flounder that Piccard and Walsh see in the deepest part of the world, have eyes? If this creature lived under 35,000 feet of perpetual darkness, why did it need eyes?

Actually, their question was answered back in 1735 by America's noted patriot, Benjamin Franklin. It was he who suggested that many fish have their own built-in electric light system. You have probably never visited the abyss, and of course, neither had Ben, but you've surely seen these magical lights at night on the surface waters. "Florescence," sparkling flashes of light on disturbed surface waters, Ben Franklin concluded, was caused by microscopic sea organisms, "the luminescence of living things." Today it is called "bioluminescence." Most marine biologists are now convinced that of the thousands upon thousands of creatures that live in the abyss, most of which no one has yet seen, almost all are bioluminescent, and although their vision may be poor, they can see the various flashes of light from other fish and instinctively know whether these fish are friend or foe, are something to eat, or something that will eat them. Thusfar, over 1,000 different sea creatures that have been captured from the depths beyond 1,000 feet have been categorized by biologists as being bioluminescent. One ugly five-inch creature found in small schools at a depth of about 1,500 feet in every ocean in the world, is the hatchet fish. Its skin is made up of a silvery iridescent pigment, and it has light producing organs imbedded in its skin as well. The hatchet fish can control these lights to blink on or off through its nervous system. Some hatchet fish twinkle blue while others emit a red glow, but why the different colors, no one knows yet. The hatchet fish is aptly named, for its body is thin and sharp at the edges, shaped like the blade of a hatchet. Its big eyes are always looking upward, which probably means that its food filters down through the waters from above.

The deep sea krill and shrimp, like the ones Bebee saw glowing through his bathysphere window, light up the abyss like a swarm of fireflies, using little candle-like organs attached to their stomachs that flicker red and purple. There are long-legged crabs that clutter the deep sea bottom. They have big eyes and live in snail-like shells that are covered with luminous anemones. These crabs also have lights on their stomachs to guide them through the darkness. The anemones, called sea-pens and sea-fans, are glowing polyps that give off waves of multicolored flickers, lighting up the sea bottom like campfires in the wilderness. One type of sea-pen, called "umbellula," provides an eerie blue or pale violet light, but only when disturbed. Other plant-like animals that illuminate the sea floor in the abyss are sea-squirts and comb-jellies. When moved by the undercurrents, they also produce waves of light, but illuminate for only a few seconds. The jellyfish "aequrea," which marine biologists believe may be responsible for much of the constant light in the abyss, has a body that is made up mostly of luminous protein.

A beautiful white lily was dredged up from a depth of 1,800 feet off the Loften Islands, Norway, in 1864. Prior to this, the forms of these lilies had been found etched into ancient rocks, and it was thought that they disappeared from this earth over 80 million years ago. Now it is known that they grow in great abundance in the abyss, and that they are not flowers at all, but animals that grow in the bottom ooze. They have chalky brittle trunks and a bushy crown of what looks like five to ten white, orange, red or green feathers, or blooming flowers. Forests of these deep-sea-lilies, called "rhizocrinus loftensis" have been seen from bathyscaphs and submersibles, their feathers waving too and fro in the undercurrent, catching minute particles of food for the trunk to feed on. They are a distant relative to the sea urchin and starfish, and like the starfish, when hauled to the surface they preserve their beauty in open air, and therefore are a prize for collectors.

Another striking rarity from the abyss is the "Venus flower basket," first brought to the surface from 1,000 feet in this century by Japanese fishermen. A member of the sponge family, the Venus is intricately designed with a lacy glass-like skeleton. They have been presented as cherished gifts to newlyweds at Japanese weddings. Like the Venus, many sponges have been fished up from as far down as 3 1/2 miles in the abyss. These sponges have delicately designed exteriors that look like spun glass, or as one biologist described them as "finely woven birds' nests." Sometimes isopods or other tiny crustaceans nest in these sponges, and the sponges grow up around them, enclosing the isopods in glass-mesh cages for the rest of their lives. Besides allowing themselves to be imprisoned, isopods of the abyss have further baffled scientists by spawning only from August to November in the Atlantic Ocean, and only from July to October in the Antarctic. The question that is driving scientists mad is, how do the isopods know when it's time to spawn? There are no seasons in the abyss!

Carl Chun, a German marine biologist, shocked his fellow sea scientists in 1903, when he dredged up from the abyss "a very terrible squid-like creature."

A giant squid in the abyss, lights up like a Christmas tree in the darkness.

It was black, with big red eyes, a white jaw, and an umbrella-like web, into which it could tuck its ten arms. It also had a pair of fins that looked like cow horns stuck into its round bulbous head. "The only thing that makes it less frightening," announced Chun, "is that it is only five inches long." A few more have been dredged up since. The most recent, caught off Durban, South Africa, was 8 1/2 inches long. It was given the name, "vampyroteuthis," or more commonly "vampire tooth," and biologists have since determined that the ugly creature is not a squid or octopus, but one of the "mesotheuthoidea" family, a group of sea creatures that supposedly disappeared from the earth 100 million years ago.

Marine biologists call animals of the abyss that they thought were extinct "living fossils" and coincidentally, on the day TRIESTE made the world's deepest plunge, Harvard College in Cambridge, Massachusetts, was exhibiting for the first time, hundreds of living fossils, dredged up from the abyss by the Danish research vessel GALATHEA. Highlighted was a large deep-sea clam, thought to be extinct for 350 million years, and a new type of angler fish with a luminous pendant in its mouth to attract other fish, like a candle flame attracts moths. Dr. Anton Braun, leader of the two year Danish expedition, named the well-preserved foot-long angler "Galatheathauma Axeli," after his ship. It has been learned since Dr. Braun's fishing expedition that the male member of this deep sea angler fish family, not only dangles a candle in its mouth to attract edible fish, but also to attract a female partner. The much larger female angler drifts alone in the depths ranging from 4,000 to 6,000 feet, carrying a lighted fishing rod, often twice the length of her body. Smaller fish are thus lured into her gapping jaws. She has two sets of teeth—one long set in her mouth and a second set at the bottom of her throat that are used to push her whole and quivering prey into her belly. She can eat any fish her own size in one gulp. If the male angler cannot find the female in the deep gloom, he either dies from lack of food within a few months or from a broken heart. Some marine biologists believe that the female helps him in his "do or die" quest for a mate by leaving tantalizing deposits in her wake wherever she swims, to help the male sniff her out. When and if the male does find her, he bites into her tough skin and holds on for dear life. Apparently it doesn't matter where the male bites her, for female angler fish have been captured with the little male hanging onto her with his teeth imbedded into various parts of her body. He, in fact, like his shallow water cousins in the angler family, is a parasite, living off the occasional scraps that escape from the gluttonous female's enormous mouth. Little else is known about their relationship, only that once they get hitched, it's til death they do part.

Considered by many to be the most important catch of the GALATHEA crew was a great sea-slug of the cucumber family. It was hauled up from 23,400 feet in the Sundra Trench. This sea-slug spends it entire life trudging slowly through the bottom mud, and swallows the mud to get minute particles of food. In order to avoid suffocation, its tail is a natural periscope, which it uses to breathe oxygen from the water above. Its body is shaped like a military tank, with many sets of little legs, which it uses to bury itself in the bottom ooze. The GALATHEA crew brought up another tank-like creature of the cucumber family from 21,850 feet in the Kermadec Trench. This little bugger had six sets of legs, and two sets of horns, front and rear, which gives it an appearance of a miniature bull, coming and going. The GALATHEA biologists learned the hard way that the horns are actually quills that contain a potent sting, and they had to use rubber gloves to handle it. They also fished up three new types of swimming cucumbers, and a bristle-footed worm from 1,000 feet. The worm was a foot long, had silky skin with white, green and red bristles along the sides of its body. When touched, sharp spines darted out of its skin, producing a long, painful sting, which courageous marine biologists again had to learn the hard way. Today, marine biologists use rubber gloves when handling all creatures from the abyss, but the sting of some of these new creatures can even penetrate the gloves.

Two little monsters of the abyss are glowing hatchet fish.

Another surprise hauled aboard the research vessel GALATHEA from 23,400 feet was a "brotulid." No one had seen a brotulid for over 50 years. The first person to see one was Albert, the Prince of Monaco, when he fished it up from 19,800 feet off Cape Verde. Today, marine scientists believe the brotulid may be the most common fish in the abyss. It looks somewhat like a codfish in size and shape, with a bigger head and a more tapered body. It has only slits for eyes, and in 1980, one was caught in the Bay of Biscay that did not have eyes. The brotulid is not related to the cod, but another common deep water creature, the rat-tail, is the cod's distant cousin. The rat-tail measures two to three feet in length and somewhat resembles the brotulid, and at times, marine biologists have mistaken them for each other. The rat-tail, however, has large eyes and lives only on the bottom of the sea, with a barbell hanging from its chin to feel out food in the muddy darkness. The rat-tail has a body that glows in the dark, and derives its name from its tapering body which ends in a long filament-like tail. No one has yet tasted this fish, but its shallow water cousin, the cod, was one of the main reasons why Europeans settled America in the early 17th century. If the rat-tail is an edible fish, it's obvious that its name will have to be changed before anyone sits down to have rat-tail for dinner.

Rat-tail, cousin of the codfish, possibly our future food supply from the abyss.

Within a few months of the TRIESTE's deepest dive, the French Navy launched a new deep diving bathyscaph, ARCHIMEDES, and in 1964, it made the world's second deepest undersea penetration to 31,320 feet in the Kamachatka Trench off the coast of Japan. At this depth, her pilot, French Naval Lieutenant Gabriel O'Bryne, spent 2 1/2 hours observing and recording the existence of strange new life forms: "Giant orange spider crabs, several feet across, luminescent jellyfish, and fire-squid, with light organs around its eyes, squirting luminous ink." On a subsequent dive in the ARCHIMEDES, 27,500 feet down in the Puerto Rican Trench, French Navy Captain George Hoot reported, "I was greatly surprised by the great abundance of life and marine growth at these depths, much of which appeared suspended in the water and remained largely uniform on the bottom."

On the day that the ARCHIMEDES made her historic dive with Lieutenant O'Byrne in command, a strange new aluminum machine was launched at

Groton, Connecticut. It began a new era in deep sea exploration, and President John F. Kennedy keynoted the event of the ALUMINAUT launching with a message to the American Congress: "Knowledge of the oceans is more than a matter of curiosity," he said. "Our very survival may hinge on it...Inner space has at least the potential of outer space..."

J. Louis Reynolds, Chairman of the Board of Reynolds Aluminum Company, agreed with Kennedy, but at the moment, he was angry at the United States government, and with good reason. He had gone to the U.S. Navy to have them help finance the building of America's first deep diving submersible, but the Navy refused, so he built it himself. The ALUMINAUT was built to dive to 15,000 feet, with the ability to remain in the abyss with a three men crew on an average of 32 hours on one dive. Although she couldn't dive as deep as Piccard's bathyscaphs, she could roam the seas wherever the pilots wanted to take her, at four knots per hour, covering a range of 80 miles. She was not only the world's first deep diving submersible, she was the first to be made of aluminum, and the first to be built for oceanographic study. Reynolds had a right to be proud, but was still furious that the government didn't have enough foresight to see the potential in deep diving submersibles over bathyscaphs.

Next to come down the ways, close behind the 51-foot ALUMINAUT, at Groton Connecticut, was little ALVIN, only 20 feet long and eight feet in diameter. Her depth endurance was 12,000 feet. She could travel at four knots, with a maximum range of 25 miles, and could remain underwater for two days without surfacing. The product of Woods Hole Oceanographic Institution in Massachusetts, she was first shipped off to Miami, Florida for test dives with the ALUMINAUT. With that completed by the beginning of 1966, she came home to New England, ready to go to work, when an unexpected and urgent call came from the White House. The American government needed ALVIN and ALUMINAUT desperately. "All hell has broken loose," said the naval commander over the phone, and Uncle Sam wanted the two new submersibles to be shipped to Spain...the United States had accidentally dropped a 20-megaton hydrogen bomb, with 1,000 times the explosive power of those dropped on Hiroshima and Nagasaki, into the abyss. The two deep diving vehicles came to the rescue and recovered the great bomb. The rescue convinced officials in Washington that deep-sea submersibles were a necessity.

One of the first pilots of another submersible, DEEPSTAR 4,000, was Ron Church, noted scuba diver and underwater photographer. One of his first missions into the abyss was for the Naval Underwater Warfare Center. He and his passenger, Wes Andrews of the Center, were to find a tripod transducer array that was earlier dropped to 1,600 feet from a surface ship. Utilizing the sub's external flood light system, Ron Church reported that, "At 1,300 feet, we saw a lantern fish, hatchet fish, hake, prawns, and squid....we flew diagonally up a steep jagged underwater mountainside, and the slope was nearly all rock, volcanic in appearance. Some had indications of manganese growing on them. A deep sea shark stole past our headlights, then suddenly, out of the darkness loomed the transducer array. Directly on target," announced Ron Church. "In less then 15 minutes we had found this needle in an underwater haystack!...We then sighted a huge vertical rock cliff and followed it," continued the DEEPSTAR pilot, "marveling at the anemones, sea fans, and colorful fish. Wes Andrews then spotted a huge octopus, but I could not see it from my viewing porthole, so I eased DEEPSTAR around, expecting to see the usual five or six inch warty ball with tiny tentacles, but instead saw a huge creature. Tentacle to tentacle it probably reached eight feet across, and was the biggest octopus I've ever seen underwater."

There was another new creature experience aboard DEEPSTAR 4,000 in the abyss a few years ago. Joe Thompson was the pilot this day, with two passengers, Dr. E. LaFond and Dale Good, of the U.S. Navy Electronics Laboratory. They were taking temperature probes at 4,000 feet in the San Diego Trench off the coast of California. "DEEPSTAR's 1000-watt lights lit up the bottom," reported Thomson, "and I noticed a gray shadow through one of the port side view-ports. Then I saw a large eye. As big as a dinner plate...A split second later I spotted a huge gill plate cover and a two-foot long pectoral fin directly behind it. The great fish appeared to be mottled brown with grayish white tipping of the fin, scales and tail. The gigantic creature was 25 feet long and five feet thick. Unlike the sightings of deep water sharks I've read about, this fish was covered with scales. The largest were toward the front and were about the size of a coffee cup. If you compare the size of the fish to DEEPSTAR's 6' 2" passenger compartment, you can best appreciate how I felt at sighting this incredible beast. The visual impact was one of watching a long speeding freight train. As it passed, I was able to catch a good view of its thick tail. It was very strange looking, with ragged caudals jutting off its end on a 30 degree angle. It was not the tail of a sea bass or shark," concluded Thompson, "but prehistoric in appearance." Neither Dale Good, nor Doctor LaFond saw the monstrous fish, for at the time of its passing, they were looking out veiw-ports of DEEPSTAR's starboard side.

Many unknown creatures like Joe Thompson's "incredible beast" abound in the abyss. There is no doubt that horrific monsters live in this nightmarish deep — never seen before creatures beyond the imagination, and possibly prehistoric beasts long ago thought extinct — maybe even the legendary sea-serpent. The great abyss will surely become the world's fishing ground, and some of its strange creatures may contain cure-alls for human diseases or ailments.

Only recently at the Galapagos Rift, tethered underwater cameras dropped thousands of feet, revealed dense clusters of six-foot white seaworms in bright red casings growing on the sea bottom. They were surrounded by concentrations of clams, mussels, shrimp and crabs, growing in the darkness where no

Red sea-worms six-feet long in white casings, grow in the black abyss where no sunlight penetrates— they thrive on bacteria.

sun penetrates. Upon further inspection by scientists, in submersible ALVIN II, it was discovered that these great worms flourish on bacteria from hot mineral water vented into the abyss from nearby caverns. Prior to this discovery, scientists assumed that plants and animals required sunlight to grow. And now it's thought that there may be other great gardens of life growing in darkness at thousands of feet beneath the surface waters.

    Biologists and other scientists are just beginning to probe this dark wilderness, knowing that there are thousands of new creatures and new species to be discovered here. To many, it is a frightening never-never land, but to the boldest undersea frontiersmen it is an awesome wonderland, filled with fascinating creatures. The abyss is truly the world's last unexplored frontier, and surely, future encounters and captures of its eerie inhabitants will even boggle the minds of our scientists and the most daring of our adventurers.

LIVING WITH THE FISHES

When scuba diving was introduced to America in the early 1950's, it was apparent then as it is now that it wasn't just another pastime or sport. Anyone who has had the sea close over him know this to be true. In the depths with the fish, your body is soothed and your mind is obsessed. There is no comparable feeling in the world above the waves.

In the heart of the sea, man looses his worries and anxieties — life becomes an awesome adventure of search and discovery, without end. One could travel anywhere in this world, but never find the beauty, enchantment and intrigue that lives and breathes, untouched by man, beneath the sea. We actually owe a debt of gratitude to our ancestors that they were unable to break the surface barrier of the sea, allowing us to be the first to experience true freedom in this grand and sprawling frontier.

Yet, already our watery environs have become a major hunting ground for scientists, engineers, businessmen and adventurers, interested in oil, minerals and other so-called treasures of the deep. As Jules Verne suggested a century ago, "The sea will become the world's medicine chest and the main source of our food supply." His predictions are coming true, but in this century man has also made the rivers, lakes and oceans his dumping grounds for human and industrial wastes.

Some are diligently fighting to stop this pollution of our undersea world, but we who spend time swimming with the fish should be the real crusaders. In past decades there were other exploiters, seemingly untouchable men who enslaved others for personal gain; unchallenged men who built factories in the name of common good, but instead created slums and ghettos for us; the unknowing and uncaring men who slaughtered great beasts like the buffalo and the whale into near-extinction. Now, they threaten the underwater world, and if we wish to save it for our sons and their sons to enjoy and wonder at, then we must continuously strive to keep it from being exploited and contaminated by every type of polluter. Scuba and skin-diving are not just sports — they offer a true and unequaled challenge; a tangible freedom of life in and love of the place where fish swim — a magical place that only we can preserve. It is our duty.

Bob Cahill

A bibliography of this book may be obtained by sending a stamped and self-addressed envelope to the publisher.

ABOUT THE AUTHOR

Bob Cahill is the author of 26 books on the undersea and American history. He is a former State Representative and High Sheriff of Essex County, Massachusetts. After graduating from Boston University's College of Communications, he served two years as a lieutenant in Army Security-Intelligence, stationed in Eritrea, East Africa, introducing scuba diving to the Red Sea area in 1958. In an official capacity while in Africa, he taught the Ethiopian Commando Team the science of scuba diving. Returning to New England in 1960, he became a scuba instructor in Massachusetts, Connecticut and Rhode Island, and a professional scuba diver for New England Divers, Inc., of Beverly, Massachusetts.

As a state legislator, Bob was a member of the Massachusetts Joint Committee on Natural Resources and the New England Commission of Sea Boundaries, plus the state's sub-committee on the problems of Environment and Ecology. He was co-founder, with Senator William Saltonstall, of the Massachusetts Board of Underwater Archaeology, and served on the Board as its Director. He was co-author of the National Geographic book, "Undersea Treasures," and author of the books, "Diary of the Depths," "Marvelous Monsters," "Strange Sea Sagas," "Finding New England's Shipwrecks and Treasures," and many feature articles on the undersea for Yankee Magazine, Skin Diver Magazine, Dive Magazine and Ocean Industry.

Author Bob Cahill (left), creator of the New England Pirate Museum in Salem, Massachusetts, stands with Captain Sam Bellamy of WHYDAH fame, who drowned at Cape Cod in 1717.
Photo by Paul Bruce.